C000171388

Searching for Candy

John Candy: A Biography

Tracey J Morgan

To my brother Steven,

We'd have more luck playing
pickup sticks with our butt-cheeks

Happy Birthday

Love from Lee x

Searching For Candy

All rights reserved. No part of this publication may be reproduced, distributed, or transmitted in any form or by any means, including photocopying, recording, or other electronic or mechanical methods, without the prior written permission of the publisher, except in the case of brief quotations embodied in critical reviews and certain other noncommercial uses permitted by copyright law.

The publisher/author makes no representation, express or implied with regard to the accuracy of the information contained in this publication and cannot accept any responsibility in law for any errors or omissions.

Copyright of Tracey J Morgan 2019

A catalogue record for this book is available from the British Library

ISBN 978-1999653316

Design by Gary McGarvey youresomehorse.com

www.searchingforcandy.com

This book is about one great man,

and is dedicated to two others who are no longer with us,

Derek Morgan and Jon Hall

"No one is actually dead until the ripples they cause in the world die away"

Terry Pratchett

Contents

Credits and Acknowledgments

The Team

Senior Editor: Joe Shooman

Copy Editors: David Morgan and Rhys Perry

Design: Gary McGarvey @ Horse
                 youresomehorse.com

Illustrations: Portrait of John Candy and Alice the cat by Craig Mackay

Portrait of John Candy and Tracey Morgan by Mandy Odandiee

Big Thanks!

This is going to be a long list so hold onto your hats! Big thanks goes to Rhys Perry, Joe Shooman, David Morgan, Rob Salem, Gary McGarvey (Horse), William F. Govier, Mandy Odandiee, Craig Mackay, Derek Morgan, Carole Morgan, Richard Bailey, Jon Hall, the Howells (Elle, Elliot, Jake, Macy and Ad), Steve Swain, Mark Woodyatt Carolyn Scott, the Maloneys (and Maloney-Watsons), Juul 'Tits Up' Haalmeyer, Erica Shaw, Jonathan O'Mara, Glen Lovelock, Jo Reeves, Kat Davis, Lee Moore, Ella Roper, Jodie Foster, Karen Booth, Helen Hawksworth, Michael (The Green Oak Foundation), Johnny Vegas, Steven Millward, Michelle Morgan, Vincent DeSantis, Sarah Zacharek,

Kristo and Holly Keogh Jones, Leigh at JohnCandy.com, Will Dorrell, Tim Schultz, Liam Pritchard, Anthony Pedersen, Peter Pedersen, Andy Merry, Andy Tippens, the Kirkdale Smurfs, the staff at VNE Telford, Sarah Wilson, Kerry-Louise Farrington, Octopus/Caveman, Amanda Sorrento, Mike Mangone, Sheldon Sturges, Carpet Martin, Shawn Chaplin, Jason Swoboda, Paul Muscat, Alison Marrs, Robert Henderson, Outliers Por Vida, Robert Young, Penelope Clements, Sophie Young, Alfie River Young, William Ford Young, the BT man who fixed my phone line the day I was due to speak to Mr Brooks, Kemal Ahmed for driving me to John's old house, and everyone I interviewed or gave me time, you are all amazing! I know I'll have left someone out so please accept my apologies, my brain sometimes fails me.

Thanks to Freddie Mercury, who made it not weird for me to thank my furry companions; Archie, Daisy Mimi, Millie the Moocher, Harry Bobees, Tilda, Poppy Pickle the Brave, Sprooties, Cookie, Roo, Bear, Zippy Zoo and Myrtle, and to those in the sky; Parsley, Florence and my woolly buddy, Scampo.

A big hug and huge appreciation to everyone who contributed to the crowdfunder, this book would never have happened without you! This includes; Carole Morgan, Craig Mackay, Justin Evans, Simone Burton, Kat Davis, Sarah Wilson, Rhys Perry, Mick Perry, Sarah Zacharek, Steve Swain, Sara Edwards,

Shawn Bonning, Alonso Puente, Christina Kennedy, Andy Pritchard, Jonathan O'Mara, Sean O'Mara, Joan O'Mara, Richard Teixeira, Mark Darbyshire, Kevin Burgess, Maddie Jarvis, James Fisher, Kenn Stewart, Chris Ball, Juul Haalymeyer, John Brown Jnr, Steve Jones, Ella Roper, Jodie Foster, Glen Lovelock, Katie Jennnings, Reg & Pat Spooner, Rob Salem, Sarah Wellstead, Elliot & Elle Howells, Carpet Martin, Jon Anslow, Laura Gallen, Joe Shooman, Mandy Pullen, Will & Becky Dorrell and everyone at Hoo Farm, Jason Weiss, Jon Hall, Helen Hollingdale, Anita Cash, Chris Williams, Charlotte Davies, Jennifer Whitfield, Christopher D Lemmon, Kelly Shackleton, Lynette Howell, Eileen Jones, Neil & Emma Byrne, Michele Knight, Mark Corbett, Simon Whittaker, Toni Oliver, Jon Evans, Steve Oliver, Karen Booth, Chris Davies, Andrew Daley, Laura Miller, Sophie Archard, William R Wortham, Aaron Russell Mackenzie Nagy, Sorrell Norfolk, Michael Beard, Rene Riva, Millie de Leeuw, Sarah Hayes, Michael Mangone, Kris Abrams, Steve Maks, Andrew Reynolds and Robert Hotton.

Interviews

Thank you to everyone who gave me their time and memories, I couldn't have done this without you.

Jonathan O'Mara
Ken Tipton
Scott Edgecombe
Marty Weil
Robert Zittlau
Lisa Soland
Valri Bromfield
Dave Thomas
Sheldon Patinkin
Colleen Callaghan
Martyn Burke
Lorne Frohman
Catherine McCartney
Bruce Appleby
Trish Tervit
Jim Henshaw
Monica Parker
Jane Tattersall
Allan O'Marra
Bruce McNall
Lonette McKee
Catherine McCartney
Alexandra Bastedo
Malik Yoba
Rawle D Lewis
Karen Austin

Jay Underwood
Gary LeDrew
Donna Meyer
Carl Reiner
Eddie Koroso
Tommy Swerdlow
Kevin Pollak
Mel Brooks
Peter Kaminsky
Charles Northcote
Leon Robinson
Rick Lazzarini
Conrad Dunn
Mariel Hemingway
Mark Jennings
Louisa Jean Kelly
Greg Agalsoff
Tony Rosato
Martin Ferrero
Steve Railsback
Jon Turteltaub
Jill Jacobson
Larry Hankin
Brian Cooper
Ken Levine
Howard Deutch
Walter Olkewicz
Patricia Ferrero
Marie Ferrero Ribaldo
Joe Kroger
Nina Keogh

Leo Crotty

John Stocker

Juul Haalmayer

Bruce McKenna

Rob Salem

Greg Stillwell

Martin Anthony

Ted Schmidt

Caroll Spinney

Mickey Stanhope

Jim Clarke

Tim Kazurinsky

Rob Salem is a veteran entertainment journalist who spent almost four decades covering movies and television for the *Toronto Star*. Prior to that, as an actor and comedian, he studied improvisation at the Second City in workshops taught by John Candy and Joe Flaherty, and went on to work with them both on *SCTV*. He knew John well, as a mentor and an inspiration, and, later on, as an occasional interview subject. He lives in Toronto with his wife, fashion columnist Rita Zekas, and three very neurotic cats.

Foreword

The phrase "larger than life" is bandied about quite freely. But rarely has it been as true as it is when applied to John Candy.

Yes, he was physically large . . . kind of like a small building. But it was so much more than that.

He had an outsized personality; an immense talent; the biggest heart. An insatiable appetite for food and fun. He embraced family and friends with an un-restrained, all-encompassing love, and his fans always with a sincere and generous warmth.

He was indeed larger than his all-too-brief life could contain.

John always expected to die young – as his father had before him. And yet he lives on. His legacy survives him. He is there in his work, on TV and in the movies, and in the impact he continues to have on his fans.

One such fan is Tracey Morgan, who, like so many others, credits John (posthumously) with helping her through dark times. And this is what she has offered in return – a meticulously researched, unabashedly affectionate biographical homage.

The sometimes surprising story of John's short life, from childhood on through *SCTV* and film stardom, comes from a vast variety of sources – Morgan has interviewed more than 70 people here, from those who knew him best to those he worked with to those he impacted, significantly, if only in passing.

Among the former, his best pal from high school, Jonathan O'Mara; his long-time manager, Catherine McCartney; his friend and collaborator, *SCTV* co-star Dave Thomas; and that show's wardrobe wizard, who would later also dress John for *Cool Runnings*, Juul Haalmeyer (and yes, that's him fronting the Juul Haalmeyer Dancers).

It is Haalmeyer who here first refers to the hugs. "John was just one big hug," he tells Morgan. He was indeed. He was famous for those hugs. I was on the receiving end of a few of them. It was like being mauled by a giant bear, except without the teeth and claws.

I'll miss John's laugh. His contagious mirth. His unassuming charm. His game-for-anything energy. His Johnny LaRue-like largess. But most of all I'll miss those giant bear hugs.

And though I despair for the loss of all the fine work John will never give us, I am grateful to Tracey Morgan for keeping him alive in such a loving and intimate way.

Rob Salem

Preamble

Have you ever stood in an empty football stadium? It is the craziest thing. In theory it is empty yet it's so full, you can feel the passion, hear the chanting of the crowd. There is something so special about it and the residual energy is palpable, it can give you goosebumps, even if you, like me, are not a football fan. This is how I feel about John Candy (although I am a huge fan of John), especially whilst writing this book. Although we know John isn't physically here anymore he left something far bigger behind, something magical. He is in everyone I interviewed, in his fans and his work.

I am not a writer by trade, but this has been seven years in the making and it is written with love. I have worked very hard to create this biography / book of memories as a fan's tribute to him. I have been laughed at, told I am not good enough, that John's life wasn't scandalous enough and that I wouldn't get anywhere. I have also been supported, gifted time, carried when needed and generally cheered by so many. Those people have my thanks (even the naysayers – you gave me something to fight for).

John lifted me out of a terrible depression when I needed him the most. Seven years ago I had no direction, I was in a dead end relationship and really felt there was nothing left in this world for me (thank god for my late dog, I had to stay and look after him). I have struggled on and off with depression but this time was more severe than before. I revisited a lot from my childhood, both good and bad, the good included the John Candy movies that I grew up with (thanks to my brother, David, for introducing me at a young age to *Brewster's Millions* and *The Great Outdoors*). John, like he did for so many, just spoke to me and in every character he played, he bled a little bit of himself. This very human, kind, loving heart made you feel like he was your friend even though you had never met him. He always rooted for the underdog and made it ok to be so. I watched *Cool Runnings* every time I thought I could not write this and it always gave me the courage to continue.

I have so many people to thank, and indeed there is a list (a couple of pages ago), but my biggest gratitude goes to my family – my brother Dave who is a far better writer than I will ever hope to be, my late Dad who always believed in me, my Mum and Richard for going along with my hare-brained schemes. I'm indebted and so grateful to my wonderful partner, Rhys, who has listened to me for hours on end, shared my minor successes, wiped my tears and always provided a kind word of encouragement. Big thanks and love also goes to my editor, Joe Shooman, who is more patient than he is pushy and wore his kid gloves (go check out his work, for he is amazing) and Gary McGarvey for being an awesome designer and resisting the temptation to mock me when I'm being a technical dolt.

I hope I have done you proud John, you turned out to be everything I wanted you to be and more.

Peace be the journey.

Introduction (Second Preamble)

You cannot think of 80s or early 90s comedy without thinking of John Candy. Some of today's best loved films are still *Planes, Trains and Automobiles, Uncle Buck, Cool Runnings* and *The Great Outdoors*. They make you laugh and cry and think back to a much simpler time. A time where we would ride our bikes with friends, where going to the cinema was a huge event, our knees were scabby, and penny sweets actually cost a penny. If you watched a film on TV it was a family affair, no mobile phones to distract us and thank goodness for adverts, they gave us just enough time to take a comfort break or make a cup of tea (yes I am British). Many of my generation grew up with John Candy in our living rooms and I can't think of a better upbringing or moral compass for any young person. John was hilarious at improvising, a physical comedy genius, a kind-hearted, wonderful dramatic actor and loved by all - on and off the screen.

Like all of us, John also had his troubles. He was hurt too easily, taken advantage of, became a victim of grief, insecurity and later on anxiety. I will touch on these subjects, however they do not make a life – I will not wallow in them nor build them up to be a tragic story, they just make him human and I felt it was important not to make a mountain out of a molehill, but likewise not to ignore them.

Throughout the book I usually refer to John as 'John', occasionally flipping to 'Candy', especially where John Hughes is concerned as the whole thing would just get confusing.

I have interviewed over seventy people for this book, friends and colleagues of John's and I hope I have given the best 360-degree view I could. There are also many interviews I just could not get and for everyone who said "no" I understand, I wouldn't speak to an unknown writer about my closest friends or family either. To those who did trust me, I'm truly grateful beyond words. Thank you to everyone who helped me along this journey, every interview, lead, word of encouragement and pledge on crowdfunding. This would not exist without you and I will be forever grateful.

Mexico

At the beginning of 1994 John Candy was in Durango, Mexico filming the spoof western, *Wagons East*.

Durango, located in North West Mexico, was known as "the land of cinema" during the 1950s right through to the 80s, with credits in over 120 films. It was a favourite with film directors and producers because of its natural beauty, John Wayne spent so much time filming there he even acquired a ranch in the state. Durango can boast titles such as *Butch Cassidy and The Sundance Kid*, *How the West was Won* and *The Sons Of Katie Elder* on its resume, so Durango was an obvious choice for a Western setting.

John co-starred with fellow comedian Richard Lewis, Robert Picardo (*Star Trek: Voyager*) and Ellen Greene (*Little Shop of Horrors*). The film was directed by Peter Markle for Carolco Pictures. Carolco was an independent film production company that could boast films such as the first three *Rambo* movies, *Total Recall* and *Terminator 2*. Although they had huge Hollywood success it came at a cost, they would pay millions of dollars for their lead actors and would also make small-budget arthouse films, many of which would haemorrhage money.

By 1993 Carolco were in financial trouble. They had previously made a deal with John to work on one of their films for US$2 million, the contract was nearly up so if they didn't put John in a role they would lose their money... enter *Wagons East*! As it turns out Carolco would go bankrupt less than two years later.

Apparently, John didn't want to do this film, but due to contractual obligation he went ahead. He was hoping his fee would enable him to take some time out and focus on directing for a while after enjoying his directing debut with *Hostage for a Day,* a TV movie (which we will talk about later). Prior to leaving for the job, he rang his friend Maureen O'Hara and told her he was concerned as he felt "Something bad was going to happen in Mexico".

The shooting days were long, stifling hot, extremely physical, and the altitude in Durango was high. The Western costumes were made of leather and were incredibly heavy to wear. For some of the scenes where they were passing over a river on horseback, the bulky costumes were also accompanied by a wet suit underneath.

It was obvious to some that during this time John was in a lot of pain, although he never complained. The crew had noticed John was uncomfortable, he would stand differently until 'action' was shouted and then he would ignore the pain and act his heart out – it is one thing to act and play a character well, but to act and pretend you aren't in pain at the same time must have been exhausting. Chronic pain is exhausting.

A common theme you will find throughout this book, is that, unsurprisingly, everyone loved working with John. He had a knack of just getting on with people, they felt welcome and safe in his presence and he got on well with crew and cast alike. He appreciated everyone was far from home and according to boom operator, Mark Jennings, "He would throw a party every few weeks, each time having a mystery bartender - which of whom was always John dressed up as somebody different. He gave all the ladies a box of chocolates and a dozen red roses on Valentine's Day and not to leave the men out, he gave them each twelve glow-in-the-dark condoms".

Costume dresser, Donna Meyer, recalled, "On Ash Wednesday we were going to be shooting an hour or so out of town. He knew that most of the Mexican crew were Catholic and that with our very early morning calls and long days, most of them would not be able to get to church. So he made arrangements with the Priest of the church he had been attending, to travel out to where we were shooting to bless and give ashes to any of the crew members who wanted it. It was the most thoughtful thing I'd ever seen."

As much as he tried to make everyone happy, Dave Thomas, an old compadre from the Toronto Second City comedy troupe, told me that John wasn't having the best time there, '...and John could have a good time wherever he was'. He was also reported to have told hotel staff that he was tired and he just wanted to go home and see his family.

At the end of a long day on 3rd March 1994, just a few days before shooting was due to finish, John rang his co-stars to tell them how pleased he was with the scenes that day, he made a spaghetti dinner for his assistants and went to bed. In the early hours of 4th March John Candy suffered a massive heart attack. Personal Assistant Frankie Hernandez received no response to wake-up calls, so he broke into John's apartment. He found John half on, half off the bed like he was putting his shoes on.

He was gone.

The world was shaken, his family and friends devastated, his fans left in disbelief.

However, luckily for us, legends like John Candy never really die.

This is part of his story.

The Beginning

Canada is often referred to as the land of immigrants, something the country has always been proud of. In fact when Canada became a country in 1867 their first ever Prime Minister was an immigrant from Scotland, Sir John Alexander McDonald. In 1937, John Buchan (Governor General of Canada from 1935-40) said immigrant groups, 'Should retain their individuality and each make its contribution to the national character', a philosophy that has actually been carried forward and today can be found in Canada's Multiculturalism Act.

In June 1913, Charles Archibald Sidney Candy left London for a new start. He departed from Avonmouth, Bristol, UK, via The Royal George passenger ship and emigrated to Quebec. His intended occupation was as a farm labourer. Charles' wife, Jessie Maud Mary (nee Banks) – who liked to be known as Maud - along with their sons Jack (11), George (10), and daughter Dorothy (7), were soon to follow him on 25th October 1913 via the Royal Edward passenger ship. The gruelling journey would take just under three weeks.

Two years later the Candys were settled in Toronto and Maud would give birth to another boy, Charles, and in 1917 they would have their final child, another son, Sidney James Candy.

An unusual name, 'Candy' is actually of old French origin, it made its way over to England, after the Norman Conquest in 1066. The origin of the name is a little unclear, although there are suggestions it could be a topographical name for someone who lived by a water channel, 'conduit', a 'conductus' that eventually evolved to Condi, Cundy, Condie, Candi, Candie to Candy. There may also be a locational explanation if someone was from Conde in France (although personally I like conduit - for later on John would certainly be a 'conduit' for laughter).

Whilst the Candys had moved to Canada, another significant family were emigrating from the Ukraine. Although the precise dates are hard to find, Frank Michael Aker and Jozefa Stefaniuk (or Josephine as she was known) met and were married in Manitoba, Canada in 1916. Frank had several jobs including stationary engineer (sometimes known as an operating engineer) and labourer, and Josephine was a stay at home Mum to their six children, Elizabeth Anne, Clarence Walter, Evangeline, Frances, Ken and Barbara.

Eventually two worlds collided: Sidney Candy and Evangeline Aker would meet, fall in love and get married in February 1946 at St Peter's Church, Bathurst Street, Toronto.

1950 was quite a year for Canada; the baby boom was in full swing after World War ll had finished in

1945, in January the first non-stop trans-Canada flight was made and in August Canada joined the United Nations to fight in the Korean War. As sport is next to religion in Canada, it's also important to mention in 1950 The Edmonton Mercurys represented the country and won the Ice Hockey World Championships. The Canadian football team, The Toronto Argonauts, also qualified for the playoffs for the first time since they had won The Grey Cup, the championship in Canadian football, in 1947.

There was also another huge highlight, however those outside of the Candy family would not realise just how magnificent this occasion would be until years later. On 31st October (Halloween) 1950 in Newmarket, Ontario, Canada, the most wonderful baby would be born. Enter John Franklin Candy. It was always a high source of amusement that Candy should have been born on Halloween, the day when children go from house to house trick or treating for candy. John was the younger brother to Jim, who was two years his senior.

A Roman Catholic, working class family, the Candys lived on a quiet street in King City. Sidney had fought in World War II serving in Germany and North Africa as part of the Scottish Regiment of the Canadian Army. According to John his father never got over his experience, he told *Parade* magazine in 1992, "He'd wake up in sweats. He bounced from job to job. He finally got his own used-car lot – Champion Motors".

Newmarket is in the York Region of Ontario, with the East Holland River running through it. A small town that grew fast in the 1950s-70s as its proximity to Toronto led to a building boom – it's located between the bustling City of Toronto and the picturesque county, so it was able to retain small town charm whilst benefiting from big city amenities. The population went from around 5000 to 11000 in this short time. It had everything - heritage, business, sports and culture.

The Candys were a happy family, but the unthinkable happened in 1955 when John's father, Sidney, suddenly passed away from a heart related problem at the young age of 38. John was only five years old at the time and as you can imagine this was an absolute tragedy for his family. How do you even contemplate something like that, let alone live with it at just five years old? John's dad had left and he didn't know why, no one explained where he had gone or what had happened. This event would haunt him throughout his life and later he would talk about it in interviews, "I didn't know why he died. I never understood it. Later, when I had kids I realised how much I missed him, I didn't have a role model."

Charles A.S. Candy (John's Grandfather) also lost his life at a relatively young age to heart problems, so it appeared there may have been an inherited heart disease or weakness.

Psychologically losing his dad would affect John for the rest of his life. Losing one's father at any age is hard, however the loss of such an important person at such a young, tender age is something that would hit anyone not once, but repeatedly throughout their life. Grief sneaks up on you when you least expect it. It's watching your friend's talk to their dad, their dad picking them up in the car, the banter, love and discipline – realising you would never have that relationship, as well as the fear that you will forget what they sound like for memories can be hard to hold from a young age. For any young person the grief can be repeated every time you see a scenario you did not experience yourself.

There isn't that much information about Sidney, however I can imagine he was a tall man (Evangeline was quite short compared to her boys), brave and courageous to have fought in the war, and to be so traumatised by the things he had seen whilst in service he must have had a heart as big as John's. If Sidney had been in service today he would have likely been diagnosed with Post Traumatic Stress Disorder (PTSD), but unfortunately back then the condition would not have been recognised nor treated. Although Sidney's heart condition was likely inherited, the amount of stress caused by PTSD would certainly have not helped.

With the loss of her husband, heartbroken but stoic, Evangeline moved her family to live with her parents in a small, post-war bungalow 217 Woodville Road, East York. Woodville Road is quite a sweet, humble street. The house, considering at one stage it gave a roof over four adults and two children's heads, was most modest, but the neighbourhood was safe and there was a real sense of community. John later remembered, "It was a very traumatic time for her. She was very young to lose her husband at that time, two young boys, very courageous. She wanted to take care of us".

East York was the only borough in Canada separated by the Don River, until 1998 when it was amalgamated into a "megacity" with Toronto. Back when John was growing up around 71% of East York was made up of English and Scottish descent. Alcohol was not served in East York restaurants until the 1970s.

Evangeline (Van) went to work at Eaton's College store, which was once Canada's largest department store, a retail and social institution with its doors open for 130 years. Whilst Van was working to take care of her boys, John was practically living in the Donlands Movie Theatre, which was a stone's throw at the end of Woodville Avenue, the road where they lived (come out of number 217, turn right and walk a hundred yards or so). He was captivated by the characters on the big screen, memorising scenes that he would act out for his mother when he got home, which she always found highly amusing. After so much trauma I can imagine it gave John great pride and satisfaction to make his mother laugh, cheering her up with his impressions and shows. Maybe this was where the comedy seed was sown? In fact looking at many of the comedy greats from around a similar time such as Gene Wilder or Robin Williams, it was the joy of making their parents laugh that led them into comedy.

John's generation also had the TV boom. Much later on in interviews he talked a lot about watching TV as a youngster, making up his own characters and putting on shows in the basement, "I have no idea how I got here. Nobody ever told me I was going to be a great comic. I did hear that I was going to turn into a TV if I kept watching it".

Growing Up

John went to Holy Cross Catholic School where he was an altar boy and later attended Neil McNeil High Catholic Boys School. Neil McNeil was a big influence on John and years later on one of his annual visits to the school he said, "My success is simply rooted in the values and discipline and respect for others that I was taught at Neil McNeil". He learned to play the clarinet (a skill which stayed with him when playing character Yosh Schmenge and Home Alone's Gus Polanski - even if he didn't play live, he knew how to imitate playing well) and was involved with the school council.

He had fond memories of school, one of which he recalled in an interview with Robert Crane for *Disney Adventures Magazine* in 1991. When asked "How old were you when you knew you were funny?" John's reply: "I think I was in high school when I became aware that I possessed a sense of humour. I went to an all-boys school in Canada and we had quite a collection of class clowns. One time the guys put someone's Volkswagen between two trees. It was impossible to get out."

It was through high school he first met his friend Jonathan O'Mara. The best friends became acquainted when O'Mara joined the dance committee as a way of getting into the dances and seeing the pop groups that played at Neil McNeil.

"You had to be 16 to get in," said O'Mara. "We had the best dances in Toronto and I met members of The Guess Who, The Box Tops, The Left Banke, Mitch Ryder and the Detroit Wheels and many hot Toronto bands." O'Mara's job was to sell socks to the other pupils, as they were not allowed to wear shoes in the gym because they scuffed the floor. "John was working with me. I liked him right away. He was light-hearted and funny and we both enjoyed mimicking the teachers, most of whom were Irish priests. We just started hanging out after that."

This friendship would be incredibly important for the next couple of years. John and Jonathan became close and were each other's confidants.

With a great work ethic from age 14 onwards John always had a job, delivering papers, working in shops, door to door sales with most of the money made going to his mother. For a while John worked in a pet supplies store. He always had his sense of humour, once when working he bumped into O'Mara's mother, in his hand he had a knife. When asked what he was doing with it, he replied in a deadpan manner that he was, "just going to trim the tails off the latest batch of gerbils".

The friends used to hang out after work as O'Mara reminisces "I worked in a convenience store on weekends and school nights. I would close up at 11, mop the floors, restock the shelves and trot around the corner to the bank to make a deposit in the night box. Many times, John would wheel in around 10:30, sit on the counter, and we'd chat as I closed up."

If the pair didn't have dates they spent Friday or Saturday evenings driving round in John's car which was an old Chevrolet nicknamed "The White Knight", they would "cruise around, talking and listening to music". There is something about driving around that helps people open up to each other, like it's a licence to be honest, John would tell O'Mara everything. "He would talk about his insecurities and his weight and often despaired of ever looking 'normal'. He would talk about his dad's heart condition and wondered if he would inherit it. His father was in his thirties when he died. Anyway, those late night drives are the best thing I remember about John. We really got into deep, personal issues. We loved the same music. I remember when Simon and Garfunkel's 'The Boxer' and 'Bridge Over Troubled Water' came out. We loved those songs. They were so depressing! They just fit."

John even taught O'Mara the art of road rage, well he tried at least…"When driving, John would often let out a stream of expletives that would make a sailor blush, whenever he was cut off in traffic. I used to marvel at this. Not being one to curse in those days, John decided I should have cursing lessons. The next traffic offence, I was supposed to do the swearing. I would let out some pretty tame stuff and

John would say, 'That's terrible, O'Mara! You call yourself an Irishman! At best, that was a D+ so shape up, mister!' It was pretty hilarious, really."

Growing up John found his love of sport; hockey, football and fishing. At high school he was on the Canadian football team, and had the nickname of "The Pink Panther". Jim Clarke was captain of that football team, he recalls "Football has two part teams. The offensive team tries to score points; the defensive team tries to prevent the opposing offensive team from scoring. I was the quarterback on the offensive team. However, John played on the defensive front line so my first impression was I was glad I did not have to play against him or be tackled by him. I always referred to John as a gentle giant. He was always good-natured with a great sense of humour. As a player John was a formidable tackler, but because of his size and weight he was assigned a front defensive line position whose goal was penetration more than pursuit."

In their Junior year they won the City Championship, the team were ecstatic! John had hopes he was heading for a career as a professional football player, with a dream that he would play for the team he had always supported, the Toronto Argonauts. Much to John's disappointment he had an accident in his Senior year which left him with a really bad knee injury, putting a stop to the professional football career, leaving John feeling down and wondering what was next. John then decided he wanted to join the forces and help in the Vietnam War.

Ted Schmidt arrived to teach the boys at Neil McNeil in the late 60s. Schmidt found it ironic that Irish priests were running the school and yet none of them wanted to teach religion, they felt their education had been second rate and they just weren't prepared to answer the deep questions kids had in the 60s. For Schmidt, that was why he was there and why he had gone into teaching in the first place, saying, "I have always been a social justice Catholic".

As well as being a religious teacher, Schmidt was also a counsellor which is how he met John. John would go in just to chat, and as Schmidt recalled, "I didn't know he was going to be famous, to me he was just a kid in his last year at High School." John would talk about his background, how is father had died young and looking back Schmidt realised that John's love for Neil McNeil was that they "were really second parents to him". Living with both his mum and Aunt Fran, John sometimes just needed to talk and tease out some of those questions that all teenagers have. With the mutual respect that was shown, it turns out this would morph into a lifelong friendship.

When John sat down and told Schmidt he wanted to go and help in the Vietnam War, Schmidt was aghast. "Usually as a counsellor you don't be too direct, you let kids come to their own decisions, but I was so horrified that he wanted to go and fight". As they were in Canada they had a window on America and they could see how ugly the war was. Schmidt had a friend who was a Marine; he brought him into the school to talk John out of even trying for Vietnam. John thought he knew what he was getting himself into as one of his uncles had died in World War 2. "I said to John, 'These are different people, this is Vietnam'. He was really appreciative of the fact I had tried to intervene, only later he realised that this would have been a catastrophe. 48,000 American and Canadian kids lost their lives, not to mention the 2 million Vietnamese".

Despite Schmidt's advice John tried to join the Marines. Even though he tried to talk John out of it, O'Mara went on that trip, "He said that basic training would trim him down and he'd get a life" (reminiscent of Dewey "Ox" Oxburger – a character John would play later in the film *Stripes*). So in March Break 1969, the friends travelled 140 miles to Buffalo, New York where John had an appointment with the recruiting sergeant, they wanted to see him the following day for a physical exam. O'Mara remembers, "The next day, we went back, having shared a bed in the motel, a la *Planes, Trains, and Automobiles*, a scene which was so similar to our experience that I think John must have had a hand in it." Due to John's previous knee injury he failed the physical and was told he "would never get past basic training." That night O'Mara pulled John out of his depression by jollying him out of it and going to the movies, they watched *Bullit* and "later, we sat through three straight showings of *Midnight Cowboy*, a great, but depressing film, one which John made into an hilarious skit, him playing Joe Buck."

Thank goodness for that bum knee.

Despite the loss of his father growing up there were a lot of happy times for John. The family were very social and liked to entertain. "We lived with my grandparents. My grandmother was Polish, so we had a lot of cabbage rolls and coffee. There was the North American diet and my Grandmother would cook that roast until it got good and gray. I never knew meat was pink until I was twenty three. Ooooo, what's this? Pink. Ooooo send it back. Boil those vegetables down. In summer there's always stuff from the garden. Take-out food. A lot of barbecues. It depends on the occasion. I guarantee you, no one ever walked into the house who didn't get fed. There were some fine meals. I look back now and that house was so small. How could twenty people fit in there? We did. There were Christmas and New Year's parties. It was great. Good memories."

A responsible John took on the father role, something which was mirrored throughout his life, looking after people and in particular, being extremely protective over his family. He was surrounded by an adoring family, a good school and plenty of friends. Women played a big role. After the loss of his father, John's Aunt Frances (Fran) lived with them for a while, his mother and her sister were inseparable, 'Van and Fran' as they were known. Surrounded by women and being a very respectful soul, John was very good at wooing the ladies, mainly because he was always unassuming and such a gentleman. O'Mara recalls "The ladies liked John because he was up for anything and very witty. He was tall and heavy set, which made smaller people, boys included, feel safe around him." Once his elder brother Jim had moved out John was the head of the household and he took that responsibility very seriously. Ted Schmidt gives a lot of credit to Van and Fran for the way John turned out.

After his football and Marines careers were no longer an option John went to Centennial College in Scarborough. With no idea of what he wanted to do he enrolled on the journalism course "because it was easier than typing", but he complained to Mr Schmidt that they were teaching him things he had learnt in Neil McNeil, so he later dropped out and joined the drama group.

As well as college John was still working part-time, now in Eaton's College Sporting Department; little did he know that this was where fate was going to smile down on him in several ways.

Fate

In 1970 Glaswegian, Catherine McCartney (who had immigrated to Toronto when she was just 19), started an acting agency right across the street from Eaton's College. Eaton's had a cafeteria; McCartney had gone over for a takeout and was standing in line when a man literally ran into her, nearly knocking her off her feet. It was John. McCartney tells me, "He felt so terrible about that, he was so worried that he had hurt me and we started talking." John and McCartney just clicked, they sat down together, chatted, and without knowing what that encounter would bring, became lifelong friends. John explained he had just finished school, was working at Eaton's part time and was taking some acting classes. McCartney explained that was a coincidence as she had just started an acting agency, at that time there were only two or three agencies in Toronto.

"Then as these things happen, the day after I was over there, he saw me, he waved and then he came over to see how I was. I said to him 'Do you still want to be in this business?' and he said 'Sure'." McCartney's agency had just got a breakdown for a TV commercial for Colgate toothpaste. The lead in the advert was a well-known celebrity, Art Linkletter, who was a Canadian born TV and radio personality, presenting several shows including *House Party* and *Kids Say the Darndest Things*. The production company wanted some young, high school football players to be in the locker room and McCartney thought John would be a good fit. As John wanted to be a football player in real life he was happy to be put forward for it, he had a picture that McCartney put in a cab and sent over for the casting team to see. "He went the following day and low and behold he got it. So that was the beginning. That was his first professional job."

So John nervously went along to his first paid acting job.

Art was in a terrible mood that day and was quite a scary prospect for any young amateur actor. John later recalled how he hated doing that job, "It was horrible". Art Linkletter had at one stage told John that he shouldn't smoke, 6ft 3 John retorted by looking down at him saying, "Yeah, it will really stunt my growth". Although not enjoyable the experience was good for John and he made another friend for life that day - Jim Henshaw.

They were both 21, John had been cast as a Lineman, Henshaw as a Running Back and there was another guy playing a Quarterback. They each had a line or two, but the main star was Linkletter, who, during the commercial would come into their locker room to explain that "Colgate protected your teeth the way helmets protected our heads".

Henshaw elaborates: "The Quarterback had done several commercials, but this was the first time for

John and me so we did the rookie actor thing of sticking close together, covering for each other and sharing whatever we separately gleaned of this new world."

Linkletter was having a bad day and according to Henshaw the Linkletter he met that day would have had most kids screaming, "Get me the f**k out of here!"

Who knows what was bugging Linkletter that day, but his mood did not improve throughout the shoot and he seemed to have a problem with everyone and everything. John had one line that he ended up saying 100 times for the amount of takes the advert took, that line was "Oh sure, Casanova!". Henshaw recalls, "John and I had never worked with a BIG star before and tried to stay out of his way. But we still became the occasional focus of his dissatisfaction. As the day wore on and we sweated under the hot lights in our equipment, it felt like it would never end."

To cheer each other and pass the time John and Henshaw talked about football. John told Henshaw how he had been a high school star player and how he had wanted to play for the Toronto Argonauts, Henshaw was a staunch Saskatchewan Roughrider fan so the banter and friendly rivalry kept them up beat.

Later that afternoon, as the crew were working hard to get everything 'just so' for Linkletter, John and Henshaw hung out in the locker room. "John and I lounged against our lockers. He wondered what really was making the man so damned unhappy. I remembered hearing that his daughter had died a couple of years earlier after dropping Acid and trying to fly out her apartment window.

"John took this aboard and said, 'A couple more hours and we'll all be looking for windows.' I cracked up. So did the crew. Even the Quarterback got it."

Unfortunately so did Linkletter (they didn't realise that their mics were on the whole time). Storming back in to the studio Linkletter demanded that both John and Henshaw should be fired, it was only when one of the production team stepped in and told him that he was going to miss his plane they got the rest of the commercial finished within 15 minutes.

Just a short time later, John and Henshaw would find themselves working together again as extras in their first film, *The Class of '44*. John played Pauly, they only had small parts and although excited to be in a film, Henshaw told me, "I don't think any of us had more than a line or two in the movie. It wasn't a great movie by any stretch. It was one of the first movies made in Toronto, it was being made because *The Summer of '42* had been so successful, but the original cast really had no interest in being there. We felt like they were just being handed work and they didn't seem happy about it and it confused us. We were just happy with our one line."

John and Henshaw were even more excited when John discovered Henshaw was wearing pants that had been worn by none other than Frank Sinatra or as the label said 'Francis Sinatra' (they were period costumes brought over by wardrobe from LA). They also found two drink tickets for the Catalina Island Yacht Club in the pocket (a popular hangout for Hollywood Stars from the 1920s onwards); they each took one as a memento.

Frequently hanging out in Catherine McCartney's office, things just kept falling into place. It was here John met a young aspiring writer, Lorne Frohman, they instantly hit it off and started writing together. John and Frohman used to have an office on Yonge Street which was above a strip club, it was one of the first generation of strip clubs that were more than burlesque in the region. Very often they would never make it to the office. "By the time we got up the first two floors of stairs we were so tired, and we smoked then and we would stop and go into the strip club. We were just like these two immature, vulnerable writers whose eyes popped out. We started at eleven o'clock in the morning and the club opened at eleven and we would never get up there, so that was a lot of fun."

"We would sneak in and watch the girls" Frohman recalls, but they would never talk to anyone as they were too embarrassed.

When they did get to the office they wrote a lot, including a show. "We went to a place in Toronto that was called CFTO TV. John and I went to pitch a show, coincidentally enough it was a show like *The Daily Show*. It was called *Eyewitness News* and John and I thought we were television producers, performers and writers, we went in to pitch the show, we weren't arrogant but we thought we knew everything."

Pitching to Gerry Rochon, a Canadian Producer, they fast learnt they that actually didn't know anything about television or the logistics of producing a programme. Rochon obliterated them. "He asked us what the budget was, how would we produce this, cameras and editors? We basically knew nothing of that, he just threw us out of his office, he said, 'Do you know what? You guys will probably never amount to anything'. The funny thing is when I bumped into John later on in life after we had gone our own ways, John did two shows out of CFTO where he was the star, just as he was becoming well known. He would walk down the hall of CFTO and every time he saw Gerry Rochon he would raise his finger and would just make fun of him and it became a standard joke. That was really funny and Rochon didn't do it as serious as it sounds, he had a liking towards us, and really and truly we didn't know what we were talking about." Frohman found John very funny, especially as they came from very different worlds, Frohman was Jewish and John of course was Catholic. Frohman would pick John up every day, he drove a Jaguar XKE convertible and in Frohman's own words, "Yes, I was spoiled. My father bought it for me to try and lure me into law school. Of course I never had the grades because I was close to an idiot but here we were driving around town in an XKE like stars and who knew we were just two jerks trying to get a break in show business which by the way, at that time, there was no show business in Toronto! I felt like a fake driving around, but Candy liked it."

John started to focus on his acting career and featured in a few more adverts including one for *Molson Golden Ale*. During the next couple of years John would also meet a sweet art student, Rosemary Hobor, via a blind date. The couple hit it off straight away, he then asked Rosemary to help type a script for him and from that day they were together, always.

Setting the Stage

In 1971 John landed one of his first roles on the stage in a production called *Creeps*, written by David Freeman and directed by Bill Glassco. The play explores cerebral palsy from the perspective of someone who is affected by the condition. John was cast as one of the two Shriners, the other Shriner was Charles Northcote. To put that into context for anyone who is not familiar with the term, a Shriner is a member of the group 'Shriners' – originally called 'Ancient Arabic Order of the Nobles of the Mystic Shrine' and is related to Freemasonry. They are known for charity work, especially for the 'Shriners Hospitals for Children'. The hospitals are part of a network of non-profit medical facilities for children with orthopaedic conditions, burns, spinal cord injuries and cleft palates.

Northcote was at University and practicing drama at the Shaw Festival in Canada. Wanting to get into the acting world professionally, he asked the wardrobe mistress "Do you know of anything going?", she advised him to give her friend in Toronto a call as they were just starting up a theatre there. Northcote put the call in and found himself at the Tarragon Theatre, which, as Northcote describes to me, is "now one of the best known theatres in Toronto, but at the time it was just starting up and the theatre was being built around us."

Up until this stage, John and Northcote had both been amateurs picking up bits of work here and there. This was one of the first times they were being paid to act on a semi-permanent basis. They had three different scenes with time to kill in-between. Northcote told me, "We were dressed as Shriners as it was the whole thing about charity and the how the characters disliked charity etc. John and I had these three scenes together and we were outrageous. I wore robes and in one scene, John had a Mickey Mouse mask where he would do a Jack Benny style take against his face with the mouse mask and looking back and forth at people. This play captured the imagination of Toronto, it was supposed to run for a couple of weeks but it kept on being extended and being extended.

"As it was extended all of us became a lot closer, the play lasted around 90 minutes so at 9.30pm we were free every night, at one of the local tavern's, The Clinton Tavern we could get 5 pints for a dollar. We would go and we were making CAN$40 a week, or I thought we were making $40 a week each – later on when John was very successful I was visiting him, he said, 'You were making $40?, I only got $35!' So I made $5 more a week than John in that first decade."

Meanwhile Allan O'Marra was dating a lady called Julia, Julia happened to be a good friend of Rose and John as they all worked at Eaton's together. O'Marra recalls, "The four of us went out together, on occasion for drinks and my first time seeing him as an actor was in the theatre production of the satirical review, Creeps, at the Tarragon Theatre, late in the fall of 1971 which I attended with Julia and Rose. I understood that he was thrilled and excited about his first theatre gig and I was highly impressed with his acting in the play, he appeared to be such a natural." Like Rose, O'Marra attended Ontario College of Art in Toronto, he actually took early head shots of John for his acting resume and would later paint a portrait that the Candy family still treasure today.

The way the Tarragon Theatre was laid out there was only one spare room that served as a dressing room. As John and Northcote had three entrances in the play that were spaced quite far apart there was lots of time for them to chat and joke around. Northcote remembers, "Well John at that point is when John became 'John Candy'. He was so funny, I remember him doing the 'International Cow Convention', held at the cow palace in San Francisco. All cows have the universal language – the monosyllabic moo – the cows from different countries had different accents. So I would interview him and I would talk to the Swedish cow – and John would 'moo' in a Swedish accent, the Hawaiian cow was called Moo-moo, the Polish cow was Oink, it was silliness. We would go to the bar afterwards and continue to celebrate really, we had fun every night, hell we were young, it was magic, we were being paid to act and we were in this hit show. So it really was a golden time."

It was a great time to be involved in theatre as it had just started to take off in Toronto, and out of that, a whole alternative theatre scene emerged.

Another memory Northcote has of John was that he was a major hockey nut. "We would watch ice time for his team – that was the first time I met Rose, his going to be wife. She, at that time was going to the Ontario College of Art, he adored her. So Rose and I would pack up thermoses of coffee etc. and we would always go from the theatre or the bar to an ice rink somewhere. It's cheaper to book time in the off peak hours, so often it was midnight. Rose and I would sit in the stands, pretty much the only people in the stands, drinking coffee and watching John play hockey. He was remarkably light on his feet, he was fast on the ice."

During that time he was working as a greeting card delivery and salesman. He would go to different stores that were on his route, check the cards and make sure that the stock was good. Northcote would sometimes go with him, "It was so funny to think after all these bizarre jobs that he ended up where he ended up, but the thing about John was he was always consistent – what you saw was what you got. He didn't put on any airs, whether he was talking to a greeting card buyer or talking to a star. That was 1970, of course we kept in touch. In '72, I got a break and I was cast at the Stratford and Shaw Shakespearean festival, John helped organise a surprise going away party for me and it was just so wonderful, a lot of friends that both of us had acquired over the two or three years, from the *Creeps* cast onwards, came to wish me well going off to Stratford, because that was a big deal."

Funnily enough John would soon be fired from his job. There were 40 salesmen and he was number 40 on the list. His boss at that time said to him, "I knew I shouldn't have hired an actor". To John this sparked something in his head and he was overjoyed, someone actually thought he was an actor!

In 1972 John met another very important lady in his life, Valri Bromfield.

Bromfield met John in a store, at that time she was doing a children's theatre production performing for children in camps and hospitals. "We were making about CAN$25 a week...I swear. So when I met John I just thought he was the sweetest, smartest, funniest guy I had ever met. He has always been warm and extremely affiliative. He made friends very easily and everybody seemed to feel loved. Well, that's the first impression of John that I recall. I told him about the theatre company and that we needed another performer. I told the director about John and very soon he had auditioned and traded in his money-making job for this fly-by-night profession. And it was hardly a profession at that point. We had a blast working together."

John joined the Caravan Theatre children's touring troupe after Dan Aykroyd turned down the role, considering himself as more of a comic.

Shortly after that John met Aykroyd through Bromfield.

"I don't recall that I introduced them but maybe I did," she told me. (She did – Aykroyd has confirmed this in interviews) I loved them both. We were all friends in Toronto at the time. All the people in theatre and television seemed to know one another. We had great parties. I lived in a store front for a while - 505 - then Danny rented it when my girlfriend and I moved out and he turned it into a speakeasy."

Little did John know that his new friends Aykroyd and Bromfield were going to bring even more opportunities and fate into his life.

John was in a few different plays around this time, he worked on several with Monica Parker, one that sprung to Parker's mind was when they were both playing scout leaders in a show, "I think that was the first time we worked together. John was really mischievous and funny in many ways, he was sort of really open, he loved a good laugh he loved to make people laugh, those early years with John were just delightful.

"He would always get to the theater at the last second, literally 10 minutes before we were due to go on stage we would be like 'where's John?', he would arrive just in time. He would come in laughing and you would forgive him - because he was John!"

1972, elsewhere in Toronto, at the Royal Alexandra Theatre, there were future members of Second City acting in the cast of *Godspell*, with Paul Shaffer directing. Everyone in Toronto was very sociable, especially those that were in the arts, they tended to meet others in the same industry very quickly. Funnily enough John wasn't in *Godspell*, which was probably just as well as he absolutely hated it. Thereafter, every party where they had the ex-cast of *Godspell*; Gilda Radner, Eugene Levy, Dave Thomas, Martin Short, Andrea Martin would all sing songs from the show and John would always chastise them for it. Aykroyd joined John with the mocking and it would become a long-standing joke between them all.

Second City

Since God was a boy, well maybe not that long ago, but certainly since the late 1800s, Chicago has been known as "The Second City", only being surpassed by New York for a larger population.

On 16th December 1959, a small capacity cabaret on the North Side of Chicago opened for its first night. There were eight unknown performers complete with props, performing improv. The first Second City comedy troupe was born. I expect that day, the performers did not realise they were setting something up that would be revered and very alive to this day, nurturing hundreds and thousands of performers and helping bring to the stage some of the biggest comedic players of our time.

In Spring 1972, Second City decided to open a troupe in Toronto that was to be based on Adelaide Street. Joyce Sloan, Bernie Sahlins and Del Close who were running Second City went to audition potential cast members.

Aykroyd and Bromfield had already travelled to Chicago to meet Sahlins and Sloan and to audition for the troupe. They advised John they were going down to the auditions and he should too. John was too nervous to put himself forward, "Every big player in Toronto was auditioning, people from *Godspell*, people from the TV, I didn't think I'd stand a chance", but John agreed to meet them at the auditions and have lunch with them both for moral support. At the time John was in a children's theatre performance of *Rumplestiltskin*.

John remembered that day, in an interview taken from *The Second City by Sheldon Patinkin*;
"I was invited by Dan and Valri Bromfield to join them for lunch. And they'd put my name on the list to audition, unbeknownst to me. And while I was standing around waiting for Dan and Val to finish their work there, my name was called. They pushed me into a room.

"I said, 'Aw, I'll kill you, I'll kill you for doing this to me'. And I went into this theatre, and I was scared. They said 'Go up on stage there. This is a department store exercise. You have to do this game. That's all we want from you'. Sweat was all over me."

During John's audition Close turned to Sahlins and said instantly that he wanted John for Second City, Close pestered Sahlins all day until Sahlins broke and said, "If you want him so much, take him to Chicago".

"Two days later they called and said, 'Would you move to Chicago?' It took me about five seconds to get my mouth open. They said 'You'll be there for a couple weeks.' I ended up living there for about a year and a half", John recalled.

John thought he was going for a very short time, so literally packed for a couple of weeks, he had never left Toronto before, he was by himself going out into the world at the age of 22 and thought "well, here we go". Not realising he needed a visa, John arrived in Chicago and was pulled aside by customs, who thought he was a draft dodger! Talking to Brian Linehan in a later interview John said, "So they pulled out this big book and they started going through the pages. And now I am frightened, I had people waiting for me, Joyce Sloan, it's been 45 minutes and I have no way of getting to them and I don't know what these people are doing. Eventually three supervisors came over to me and they were eye-balling me, the hockey playoffs were just happening, and one of them says, 'Who do you like, The Blackhawks or the Canadians?' I said 'Blackhawks' and they gave me a stamp and let me through."

In 1973 the initial Toronto group was Dan Aykroyd, Valri Bromfield, Gilda Radner, Jayne Eastwood and Gerry Salsberg, (Eugene Levy and Martin Short auditioned but they didn't get in the first time around). Joe Flaherty came over from the Chicago troupe to mentor them along with Brian Murray-Doyle (Bill's brother). In terms of comedy, the group gelled, unfortunately due to not being able to get a liquor licence, business was failing - the iced tea and Coca-Cola on offer was just not attracting the crowds. At that time in Toronto, it was almost impossible to get a liquor licence unless you were also serving food. Shortly after opening, a bailiff turned up and closed the venue down.

John on the other hand had gone to Chicago and was being shown round by fellow troupe member, Bill Murray. Bill said to John, "This is my town and this can be your town too!" He took John everywhere, as John remembered in an interview, "He took me all over the city, showed me every landmark. We'd have a hamburger at the original McDonald's, a pancake at the first International House of Pancakes. We went to every weird, seedy area imaginable." Murray also took John to his first Cubs game at Wrigley Field, where John also experienced sunstroke for the first time!

Chicago was quite the culture shock, John went from Toronto where alcohol was only served in restaurants or illicit speakeasies, to Chicago where the bars were open till 5am. John took advantage of this and like any young adult living in a big city for the first time, to say he thoroughly enjoyed himself would be an understatement.

John lived on Curly Court, which he found amusing as Curly Howard was one of his favourites from The Three Stooges, (later, Jennifer, John's daughter, would actually stay in the same apartment block when she joined Second City). After the Second City shows, John would invite the cast back to his place to watch movies. He literally knew everything about every movie, every actor - he was so knowledgeable about movies and TV shows, he just loved and respected the medium so much.

Sheldon Patinkin was an Artistic Consultant for Second City (he was SC alumni from 1959), when he first saw John up on stage it was like John was lost, he kind of melted into the background, which was really down to his lack of confidence. Patinkin told me, "We spent time on building his belief in himself, and by reassuring him that something not working but you tried, is a lot better than not knowing whether it would work or not - by not trying it, (we got him to overcome his lack of confidence) by telling him to cut out the bullshit and quit being an asshole. All because we really believed in how good he was and could be."

Patinkin moved to Toronto to help out with the troupe as an Artistic Director. His words about John may have sounded a little harsh however he was renowned for saying "It's better to be an asshole than a chicken shit", he just called things as he saw it. (Sadly Patinkin died in 2014 but I am so grateful I had the chance to converse with him.)

Turns out John would be in Chicago for over a year, before they sent him back to Canada where Second City Toronto had just been bought for CAN$2 by a man called Andrew Alexander. Alexander was born in London, UK, his family emigrated to Canada in 1951. He had a background in cab driving, journalism and the arts and was working at the Ivanhoe Theatre in Chicago when he met Bernie Sahlins. After hearing of the Toronto troupes financial difficulty, he negotiated with Sahlins to assume the Toronto theatre's debts in exchange for the right to operate The Second City in Canada, he paid Sahlins CAN$2 and took out a CAN$7000 loan from a friend.

Alexander opened the doors in 1974 at a new location, 110 Lombard Street, Toronto, the venue was a 19th Century fire house called The Old Fire Hall. He put together package deals where people could have dinner upstairs and then go to the show afterwards, hence they got their licence to serve alcohol. At this stage John was sent back to help, he was reluctant to leave Chicago, but it turned out to be the best move he could have made.

Initially John was sent to Pasadena to start up a new Second City there, in the cast was Betty Thomas, Doug Steckler, Eugene Levy and Joe Flaherty, it didn't do so well and closed within a month. Dave Thomas at that time had started working with the Second City Toronto troupe, so when John came back to Toronto, Thomas was thrilled to be working with him. Thomas remembers, "Oh my god, he was like a big kid. People who like comedy and love to laugh have that kid aspect in them. I had so much fun with him on stage and I bonded with him immediately. We had similar sensibilities could make each other laugh. We just had a really great time.

"John, when he improvised, had a thing that he described as his room and all the props and books and bookcases and guns and things like that, that were all mime and imaginary, were always in the same place. So if you did a lot of scenes with John you knew where everything was and that made it really fun because the audience at that time were returning patrons so they knew where the stuff was too. So when you went for it there would be this delightful moment of recognition with John and me on stage, and him and the audience would all share. Some of those things got really crazy and were a lot of fun.

"John was very heavy-set but he was very physically strong, he wasn't a pudge-ball. One night when Danny (Aykroyd) came back to visit the show, John picked up Danny and me at the same time like horizontally one on each shoulder and spun us around the room, until this day I can still see Danny's face sideways going round and round as John spun him. Danny and I were laughing, cos Danny wasn't a little guy and I was 180 pounds myself, that's a lot of weight to pick up! So I used to use this with John, cos John was so strong, I could run at him on stage, flip into the air and tuck my legs under like a ball and John would catch me and he would barely rock on his heels. So we would be able to do things that were physically fun. Then we would do the reverse of that, where John would let me pick him up with two fingers by his lapels, like he is pinned against the wall, and John would go up on his toes and it would look like I was lifting him with two fingers. He loved to do those kinds of things and so did I."

"Another night with John," Thomas recalled, "Our idols Peter Cook and Dudley Moore came to the show. They were both drunk and it was odd the way they were playing. But Peter said he wanted to do a scene where John was a priest and I heard them talking about it backstage and then I saw Peter get down on his knees and he was praying or something cos I was working and discussing another improv scene I was going to do. There was just John and Peter in the scene, Dudley was not in it, John goes out there with Peter. They start the scene and Peter drops to his knees and mimics giving John a blow job. Now no one laughed, the audience was shocked and it was really kind of appalling. I watched for a couple of seconds and thought 'Jesus Christ I have got to enter this scene and save John because he is dying up there by himself'. John was just trying to laugh it off, trying to push him away, he was as stunned by the silence of the audience as I was. I ran around from the house to backstage, when you enter a scene you have to enter with a joke, I don't remember what the joke was, but I knocked on the door and I looked at John's face and there was just the sweetest look of relief. Then the scene built and more people entered in. The way Dudley was playing it that night was kind of cheesy I thought, he would run in, do a line, get a laugh and run off. That's not fair, in improv you owe the scene more than just running on, getting your laugh and exiting. He did that multiple times in a scene where he would run on do a joke and then run off. He was kind of annoying, like a gnat. We both admired these guys, we know how talented they are and we were fans of everything they have ever done. I remember afterwards I was discussing it with John and he was really bummed out that your idols had feet of clay, first of all that they were that drunk and secondly that the actual level of work was that horrible. We wanted to get into the calibre of stuff that we loved in *Beyond the Fringe* and it was just awful."

John was still doing some children's TV work whilst he was performing at night at Second City. He guested as a weatherman dressed up as a superhero, in a show called *Cucumber* (Children's Underground Club of United Moose and Beaver for Enthusiastic Reporters), about a moose and a beaver living in a tree-house learning how to report on educational topics. He was also in the cast of *Dr Zonk and the Zunkins*, a children's series that also starred Gilda Radner, Rosemary Radcliffe, Dan Hennessey and Robin Eveson. Eveson played the main character, a young boy called Billy Meek. In each episode two puppets, the Zunkins, called Zooey and Dunkin would come to life out of the pages of a comic book and have adventures. The puppeteers that controlled and voiced Zooey and Dunkin were Nina Keogh and John Stocker. Aired from 23rd September 1974, three afternoons a week on CBC Children's TV, the show only lasted one season and morphed into more of a teenage show, *Coming Up Rosie*.

Keogh remembers "At the time the show was my segments with the puppets and we would do our bit with the kid we were working with, and then they would go to other segments with the comedians - the characters didn't really interconnect but we were all on set at the same time.

"I just remember coming in to the studio and being in the studio with them all. I hung around when they did their segments, you had such brilliant talent right in front of you, John, Gilda Radner and Dan Aykroyd. Danny and Gilda were going out at that time.

"He (John) was very sweet, he didn't have another side to him at all. I hung out with Rose, she was really supportive. Sometimes you work with people and there is some little edge to people, John never had that, he was like perfection of a human being. He was always gentle and kind and funny as hell. He was sweet and honourable and he really loved Rose. They were very respectful of each other."

Once *Dr Zonk and the Zunkins* finished, most of the cast went into *Coming Up Rosie*. Rosie Tucker, who was an aspiring documentary maker living in the same building as the rest of the characters, was played by Rosemary Radcliffe. Dan Aykroyd also starred as Purvis Bickle, Catherine O'Hara was Myrna

66

Wallbacker, John played Wally Wypyzypywchuk (pronounced Wippa-zippa-chuck) and John Stocker, no longer in a puppeteering role, played the elevator clerk, Dwayne Kramer.

Stocker told me, "We had a year of working together. Wally and Dwayne were the two goofballs in the show, the crazies, and that kind of translated into being good friends. For two years we were pretty much inseparable. If you were looking for John, you found me.

"He was the most gracious giving guy I've ever been in contact with. You couldn't buy him a drink, this guy he could drink, but you couldn't put your hand in your pocket, he would just override you with a great big smile.

"John had some dark moments, but he would never show them. He was the centre of attention just because he wreaked of personality and warmth in a good way. We got to a stage where we had to make a deal, 'if you buy the beer, I'll buy the scotch'. People he didn't know he would say 'I'll get that, what else to you want? Make it a double!'."

Around this time John was also playing bit parts on *The David Steinberg Show* and starred in a satirical comedy anthology film called *Tunnelvision*. A weird watch, set in the (then) future of 1985, it's about a channel that is completely devoid of censorship.

In 1976 John had one of his first proper movie roles in a film called *The Clown Murders. The Clown Murders*, a horror film directed by Martyn Burke, follows the story of four young men who dress up as clowns on Halloween to kidnap a businessman's wife to prevent him from closing a business deal. The plan goes wrong and in a turn of events the group find out they are also being stalked by someone dressed as a clown.

Burke was looking for someone to play the part of Ollie, he told me, "There was a Canadian Comedian by the name of Al Waxman, who said John Candy is the only person who could play this role. I had never heard of John so I went to see him at the Old Firehall, Second City and he and Dan Aykroyd were a team. Aside from the overall ensemble of the cast they were kind of a team together and they were truly brilliant, they would do the improv part where the audience would throw out suggestions as to what they should make into a comedy routine. It was just breathtaking. So that's where I met John. John was shy, truly decent human being. He did *The Clown Murders,* whilst learning on the set. I am going to say what everybody will say, everyone loved John, he was a terrific guy."

The Times They are a Changing - All Aboard to Melonville

In 1975 and 1976 John co-starred in two films, *It Seemed Like a Good Idea at the Time* and *Find the Lady* respectively. He played the same character in both films, Kopek, who was the dim but sweet assistant of Detective Broom (played by Laurence Dane). Although neither film was great, John certainly got to perform and excel wonderfully in some physical comedy scenes and work alongside some legends. There is one scene in *Find the Lady* where John shows influences of The Stooges and Buster Keaton, with great physical comedy falling around in an office, a catalogue of disasters that literally destroys the whole room with clumsiness. Not only was he co-starring alongside Dane, he was also working with Peter Cook, Mickey Rooney, Dick Emery and in the case of *Find the Lady*, the beautiful Alexandra Bastedo. Sadly Bastedo passed away in 2014, but I did get to speak to her for 10 minutes on the phone back in 2012. She told me, "To work with he was very professional, with his lines, moves, he would keep the atmosphere on set quite light because he was such a jokey person. We would often go out to bistros with our mutual friend, Peter Thompson, who was a film and commercial director, in fact Peter first introduced me to John by taking me to Second City. John got on well with Peter Cook, in fact everyone got on well with everyone else, the only one who didn't mix with anyone was Mickey Rooney".

1975 also saw the arrival of the great American show *Saturday Night Live (SNL)* a live variety show with comedic actors performing sketches and improv, created by Lorne Michaels. Several of the key players from Second City ended up leaving to join *SNL* including Gilda Radner, Dan Aykroyd and John Belushi. Bill Murray joined them in their second season.

This left Second City with openings for new players. Dave Thomas took over Aykroyd's role which meant he got to work even more with John. The birth of *SNL* left Andrew Alexander, Bernie Sahlins, Joyce Slone and Del Close a little twitchy, as they were worried all their talent would be snapped up by *SNL*, so they needed to think of something to keep their own troupes happy.

Alexander was dubious about going into television, Sahlins had been bugging him to do it for a couple of years. Once *Saturday Night Live* came out Alexander changed his mind and felt they needed to, after all they didn't want to lose all their talent to *SNL*. Meeting with Allan Slaight, who was the owner of *Global TV*, Slaight told Alexander that he could give them a studio and crew if he could come up with the rest of the money. Len Stuart became a business partner of Alexander's and put up CAN$35000 ($5000 per episode). Stuart brought both secure financing and business acumen to Second City, apparently his motto was "no problem" and somehow the problems always seemed to work themselves out.

The premise of *SCTV* was a small TV station set in a fictional town called Melonville, it would follow a day's programming on a very small and cheesy broadcasting channel. They would portray the characters working at the station, snippets of TV shows, skits and adverts. The initial cast consisted of John, Dave Thomas, Catherine O'Hara, Eugene Levy, Joe Flaherty and Harold Ramis. Ramis was also the head writer at that time.

SCTV is where John thrived, he always looked back at this and his Second City days as the golden years, the chemistry between the cast was electric, they all supported each other and they were able to be as creative as the budget allowed. Everyone would contribute to the writing meetings and come up with new characters. Later this would cause a few problems as Thomas explained;

"When John was at *SCTV* he was kind of lowballed as a writer. We got our cheques one month and John said let me see what you got and I just tossed him my cheque so he could see it and it was different to his and he got really pissed off and he didn't forgive Andrew for that for a long time. Andrew was just trying to save money and John didn't contribute as much as a writer on one level. The irony of it, Harold

Ramis, who was head writer at the time, used to say people would write their sketches and bring them in the next day and John would bring his ideas scribbled on the back of a cocktail napkin. But what Harold didn't have time to elaborate in that quote was that what was on that cocktail napkin was often better than the rest of the work that the rest of the people had stayed up all night working on. John's concepts were great, they were brilliant! For example, the idea at the beginning of *SCTV* of throwing all the TV's out the window, that was John's idea and a lot of people forget that. That was really funny, John would think of those things and it would be signature, that particular image was played on NBC's worldwide sports because no one on television had ever seen it where you threw out multiple televisions from a high rise building. It caught on, you would call it a viral thing today. John had the ability to come up with these viral concepts that you went 'Oh god that's great'."

Although *SCTV* had only just started, in 1976 Chevy Chase left SNL and Michaels was on the lookout for his replacement. Flaherty, Thomas and John were invited to Michaels' hotel to meet with him, they were going to have a chat in the day and in the evening Michaels was going to see their show. Thomas remembers, "Even though *SCTV* had started, Andrew Alexander had a responsibility to respect and service *SCTV*, we went and said to him, 'Lorne is coming here to see us and steal us from your show and we really want to do it, will you let us do it?' And he said 'Yeah Ok.' That's pretty gentlemanly, I have the greatest respect for Andrew Alexander for things like that he has done over the years.

"Lorne shows up late because he always does and everybody wanted the job so much it put too much pressure on them, it was the worst improv set we ever did, it was just terrible. John wanted this job really badly, there was an aspect of John that was 'Johnny La Rue'. Johnny was big and competitive, he ordered limos when he couldn't afford them, he loved being a big shot. That was as important to him in many ways as the work, to be recognised for the work and be able to live the good life.

"So this was an important thing for John, and after the horrible show we went to Lorne's table and I waited for Lorne to say something to me and he didn't say anything, so I just said 'well alright, thanks for coming' and I left. Joe told me he left right after that. John stayed to talk to Lorne, and after an agonising several minutes of silence whilst Lorne just kind of stared at him, Lorne said to John 'Don't give up your day job'. John never forgot that, that cut John so deeply and wounded him so badly. I'm sure Lorne meant it as a joke, but John was mortified and left totally crushed. Now this is another part and another side of John, things like this would hurt John and John would carry far more of that hurt home than any of the rest of us. It was more important to him because he exposed himself and put himself on the line in a bigger way than either myself or Flaherty did. I was very guarded, I would rather give up a job than get it if it meant exposing myself. I saw that in John and it hurt me that John was hurt like that. Cut to almost ten years later, we are in New York and John came on *SNL* as a guest. John still remembered that, but he was like ah yeah I guess it is time to let that go."

This was actually where Bill Murray joined *SNL*: he was Chase's replacement.

Throughout his whole career John liked fairness, everyone should be treated the same no matter who you are. He often fell out with Alexander over money, looking back Alexander was just trying to keep everyone's heads above water, but I love the fact that John wanted everyone to be treated equally. During one of the late night shoots at Global TV the crew were served *Swiss Chalet*, John went crazy, he couldn't believe that one of the executive producers owned a restaurant and was serving *Swiss Chalet* to the crew (*Swiss Chalet* was and still is a restaurant, at the time it was one of the few restaurants to do take away food). John was incensed as he figured the crew deserved more than run of the mill take away food (the cast were obviously being served something else of a higher quality) and showed a rare moment of anger and punched a hole into his dressing room wall. Now

John wasn't a food snob, as Jonathan O'Mara told me one of their favourite haunts when they were at school, "Was a greasy spoon just up from the school called *The Alpine*, or as we affectionately named it, 'The Armpit'. It deserved that moniker." But what had upset John was that the crew was being treated differently to the cast (later on John would become quite fond of Swiss Chalet as they catered a movie he was working on). When John had calmed down, Alexander drew a frame around the hole he had punched in the wall and made John sign it, it was left for years but sadly it has now been patched up.

Some of the characters John played on *SCTV* were Mayor Tommy Shanks, the corrupt and laidback Mayor of Melonville, Harry the Guy with the Snake on His Face, the owner of a chain of adult stores, Mr Mambo - whose reaction to all the world's problems was to "Get up! and Mambo!", Dr Tongue , and the infamous Johnny LaRue. Johnny LaRue was one of John's most loved and well known characters from that era, wearing his signature 'JLaR' burgundy smoking jacket, LaRue was a sleaze, incredibly flawed, but you couldn't help but like him. There is actually a Christmas episode of *SCTV* where LaRue was doing a show called *Street Beef* - where he would rove around the streets finding out what people were up to. In the Christmas episode there was snow on the ground, the streets were deserted and the bars were shut. LaRue ends up firing the crew and doing the most amazing soliloquy on the snow covered pavement. All Johnny LaRue wanted was a crane shot - but he was always told it was too expensive, at the end of his breakdown, Santa turns up and gives LaRue the crane shot he had been longing for. Juul Haalmayer remembers that night and told me how cold it was, how they had to keep John warm by giving him brandy, funnily enough John wanted a convoy of tanks for this scene, but they couldn't afford it. John also did fabulous impressions including Orson Welles and Divine.

In the early days of *SCTV* John was also helping out at Second City, teaching workshops, this is where Rob Salem met him, Salem remembers;

"I briefly entertained the notion of being an actor, until I realised that I was terrible. I was taking Second City workshops and at the time Joe Flaherty and John were teaching, so it was great timing, talk about two great comedy mentors. John was really championing me, he really was a mentor and one of the few people at all that thought I had any talent. I would have done anything for him. At one point he suggested I try stand up comedy, which I think was his way of saying you don't work well with others. But he did point me in that direction and I did do stand up for a couple of years. It stood me in great stead because I do a lot of TV and radio stuff and that kind of stand up experience, coupled with the improvisational skills I learnt from John, I could do anything. I am not afraid to be in front of people or cameras, it gave me the tools to do what I do and expanded my journalism beyond print. I got those skills from John."

Oh, and Salem has a John and Robin Williams story! "I will tell you how I experienced it. I was taking the workshops and this was in a period when John and Andrew (Alexander) were at odds about something so John had to leave in the middle of the class. He had brought with him to the class some guy that none of us knew, this was before *Mork and Mindy*, I think Robin had shot the *Happy Days* episode which led to the pilot for *Mork and Mindy* but it hadn't aired yet. He and John had met and become friends.

"Robin was something of a small phenomenon on the stand up scene but the public hadn't really heard of him yet. So in walks John to this class with this guy – a strange looking hairy man and said 'this is my friend Robin from LA'. At one point when he (John) had to leave I heard him say 'Rob take over the class'. So me and Robin Williams are standing there and we don't know who Robin Williams is. It was that type of class that was so competitive and everyone resents everyone else. So he could have meant Rob or Robin, but we decided we would just do it together. We started demonstrating one improv exercise where you have to paraphrase, so he says a whole bunch of stuff to you and you have to paraphrase and say it back to them. So he started saying a whole bunch of stuff about himself, 'Well I went to Julliard blah blah blah blah blah' and we went from dislike to seething hatred of him, who is this asshole? Then we went onto another exercise where every line we said had to be a question and if you screwed that up you had to perform a stage death. So Robin was going to demonstrate the stage death. He started off as Peter Lorre and then suddenly gets stabbed from behind and suddenly becomes Sydney Greenstreet who stabs him, who then gets shot by Humphrey Bogart who then gets shot with an arrow through the head and it just goes on, endless impressions and characters, one after the other after the other and we went from that seething hatred to jaw dropping awe. Then he started doing his Shakespearean stuff and that was just off the wall. John was one of the first ones to see that in Robin, again he just had that knack in seeing talent in people. Six months later *Mork and Mindy* hit.

"John liked to surround himself with talented people, he was very much about fostering talent in other people, that is what made him tick. More so than the most magnanimous human beings, this was a key part of John's personality. I don't know how much of that mentoring he had in his own early life and think part of that was to do with it too."

Something In the Water?

Let's take a moment to reflect. So looking at the Second City crew you could be forgiven for thinking something was in the water around that time, John, Eugene Levy, Catherine O'Hara, Dan Aykroyd, Martin Short, Dave Thomas, Andrea Martin, Gilda Radner et al, so many talented and funny individuals coming out of Canada. Well part of me thinks that there was a little bit of magic to these times, but also the cultural shifts would have helped things along.

Of course a lot of these performers and artists were Baby Boomers, i.e. part of the generation who were born after World War 2 when there was a massive increase in births. For some reason Canada's boom was bigger than most countries, roll on 20 years and the baby boom generation are so large in numbers that they were hard to ignore. If they wanted change then people had to listen to them, and change they got.

The 60s were a time of free love, everyone was becoming more liberal. In the late 70s Toronto transitioned fast. It went from being quite a sleepy location, to an exciting, busy metropolis, alcohol was introduced into bars, people started to have a good time.

These stars grew up with TV, as TV progressed and more channels were broadcast, trends and fashions spread faster than ever. Before now a trend in

America would take a year or two to bleed into Canada, thanks to TV the changes were becoming more instant. It's not a surprise that the kids who were brought up on TV, dreaming about shows and creating their own sketches, would then go on to produce *SCTV*, a skit on many of their favourite shows.

It was like people had been given permission to try different things. I remember at University one of my lecturers, Phil Saxe, told us, once one of us had a little success those they hang around with would get a little success too, before you know it you are all climbing a ladder together. Well I honestly think this is true for John and his friends, they nurtured each other, gave themselves a safe space to try out new material and if they failed they held each other up. They literally paved the way for all future Canadian comedy, what a time to be alive.

Magic indeed.

Hollywood Calling

In 1978 the writing career of Harold Ramis started to take off, and Andrew Alexander rented a house in Bel Air so the other cast members of *SCTV* could be close and on hand to all write together. They would write in the mornings and hang out in the afternoons. Someone had an idea to have a party at their rented house - it started off with 50 people in attendance and ended up with 500! Everyone was there, movie industry moguls, musicians, in fact most of the creative echelon from the area, including Steven Spielberg. This was the first time John met Spielberg, apparently Spielberg was waiting at the party to talk to John, John didn't believe it, he thought everyone was just drunk. Turns out Spielberg did want to speak to John about playing a part in his next film *1941*, John's opening line to Spielberg was, "I liked your movie about the fish" (meaning *Jaws*). John didn't take Spielberg seriously at all, luckily Spielberg was not perturbed. During that party the members of *Saturday Night Live* turned up, Chevy Chase included. John thought it would be funny to put Chase into a headlock and walk around the party with him like that, after so long Chase protested that it was no longer funny, the more he protested the longer John held the head lock - reports from party goers say Chevy was in that headlock for over 2 hours!

1978 also saw the creation of *The Blues Brothers*, a sketch on *SNL* by John Belushi and Dan Aykroyd, under the character names of Jake and Elwood Blues. John was cast in a film called *The Silent Partner*, the lead was Elliot Gould, who played a bank teller that anticipates a robbery and steals the money himself, only for the robber to then come after him. John played a small part of Simonsen, who was also a bank teller. If you watch the film notice when John is on the phone in the background, he's apparently actually on the phone as the lines worked, placing bets during filming (he wasn't the only one, they were all at it).

1979 was a great year for John, he finally married his long term sweetheart Rose at St Basil's church on 28th April. Tony Rosato, one of John's friends and colleagues told me "One of my favourite memories about John was when he was getting married, his jacket was a little too wide so he had it pinned up a bit, so we were trying to pick up his suit and pick up flowers and so on, and it was such a special day for him he was so excited, so full of life and love, it was a special morning." Sheldon Patinkin was also at the wedding, he had previously been living in the house that John and Rose were now frequenting, so Rose stopped on her way down the aisle to see if he had picked his post up. Rose was the most beautifully stunning bride. I can only imagine what a heartfelt event that was. John couldn't have been prouder.

John also landed a small part in a film called *Lost and Found*, starring George Segal and Glenda Jackson, directed by Melvin Frank. Frank loved John's face so much, but he wanted him to play a French car rental salesman in his 50's! John tried to grow as much facial hair as he could at the time, the makeup and hair department decided they were going to give him a perm and dye his hair black, John went along with it as they told him it would wash out. It didn't. The perm took a while to relax and the dye washed out in stages so at one point his hair was purple, then pink! The film was a flop, but John's short scene is worth catching.

Despite his drunken nonchalance, John must have impressed Spielberg at that party, as shortly after they met he was actually cast as Private Foley in Spielberg's first attempt at a comedy film, *1941*. Co stars included Dan Aykroyd, Treat Williams, Nancy Allen, John Belushi (although they were never in any scenes together), Frank McRae, Mickey Rourke and Walter Olkewicz. The film depicts the panic in Los Angeles after the attack on Pearl Harbour in 1941. Since its release *1941* has gained a cult status, however at the time it was neither critically nor financially successful.

Walter Olkewicz played Hinshaw and originally was only meant to be working on the movie for one day. He was cast as a mechanic in a scene where he was working on the tank that the squad were going to drive away in. However he impressed Spielberg that much that he was kept on for the whole movie.

"The film was filmed as a covered set, which means they are filming outside but if it rains they have a place to go immediately inside to film", explains Olkewicz, "so we were in the covered set and Spielberg said to us, 'You just work something out, I want there to be a big fight going on'. I said 'John you over here, Frank you over there'. Because I was a director of my own comedy group at that point, I was inspired by these people, but I was in no way intimidated by them, so I took over. Spielberg came back and of course I was a major part of this thing I had created. Spielberg said 'well you are very good, do you have any plans for the next few weeks?' the crew and cast applauded as they knew that I had just been upgraded from a day player to an integral part of the cast."

So Olkewicz was part of the tank crew, alongside John, Rourke, McRae and Aykroyd. Olkewicz was literally with John every day for 28 weeks and they were in every scene together. They also spent a lot of time hanging out on set and getting to know each other. Olkewicz reminisces, "Working with him, we always had these little games that we played. We played baseball games with little pencils, we would make noise and wave our fingers like the crowd was cheering. We would sit around on set for four, five, six hours before you do an hour on camera.

Spielberg, as wonderful as he was, and he was wonderful, would wait till the cloud formation was exactly right in the sky. So we would sometimes have to wait hours just to get a shot in."

One of the initial traits that struck Olkewicz about John was that he was a man of great integrity. The set was full of beautiful women and lots of the cast were cheating on their wives and girlfriends because they could.

This was Olkewicz's first feature film, "I was kind of in awe of it (the affairs) and I remember going to John and saying 'Wow this is great!' He said, 'Ya know I got my girl at home and why would eat hamburger out when I have steak at home. I got my Rosie.' I thought wow! Not only was he not tempted by it he couldn't even see any logic to do anything like that, and I tell you some of the big people were having girls going in and out of their trailers. So it was not only tempting but also pretty easy to hide. So we talked about that a lot, what Rosie was like. 'That's my bride, she will always be my bride' he would say."

During their time on set John, Olkewicz and McRae discussed their weight as they were all big men and they decided that they all needed to lose weight. So they made a bet. John and Olkewicz both had to lose 50 pounds and McRae had to lose 100 because he was bigger and he couldn't even weigh in on scales anymore. So whoever won the bet, the other two would have to buy the winner a US$500 suit.

However a year later they all ran into each other "John had gained about 80 pounds, I had gained 50 pounds and Frank was off the scales."

By 1980 John was starring in a couple of smaller films, a Canadian production called *Double Negative* and also a TV film, *The Courage of Kavak the Wolf Dog*. But things were about to get interesting when Aykroyd and Belushi had written and were making a movie of the *Blues Brothers* (a progression from their *SNL* characters). A star studded affair featuring; James Brown, Aretha Franklin, Ray Charles, John Lee Hooker along with other amazing blues musicians, Carrie Fisher as Elwood's estranged ex-girlfriend and John Candy as the role of Burton Mercer - the parole officer trying to track the brothers down. Directed by John Landis the film was an amazing success and still holds up well today. Candy's character had a small, but legendary part which he played beautifully. In fact you will find many people still quote his famous line when ordering drinks "Orange whip? Orange whip? Three Orange whips". If you have ever wondered how to make an orange whip, just add vodka, rum and cream to orange juice, pour over ice and stir (I hope it tastes nicer than the recipe sounds!). I'm sure John used Orange Whip as it's the last thing you order, and it's much funnier than ordering three beers.

For John, his personal life was also going well, he and Rose were expecting their first born. John had it hand-written on his *Blues Brothers* contract that should Rose go into labour whilst they were filming that he could leave straight away to make sure he was by her side. On 3rd February 1980, the beautiful Jennifer Candy came into the world, John was beside himself and adored being a father. That year John also bought a country estate in Queensville, just outside of Newmarket and around 40 miles from Toronto. He told David Letterman in an interview, "I was sitting on the toilet one day, looking at the want ads. I wanted to get out of the house I was living in, and I saw this great country estate, ten acres, pond, barn. The price was right, I shouted 'Rose, honey! I've got it'." John went down there the same day, it was in the middle of a snowstorm and bought it, "No Real Estate agent, I didn't notice the running water".

When they moved in they realised there was water running right through the property, he had to pay to have a channel built around it to divert the water, then his grass went brown so he had to pay for an irrigation system. This makes me chuckle as it's so John, he rushes in to live the dream and gets so caught up he doesn't check out the practicalities. He spent the next three years making movies trying to pay for the place. Of course it all worked out and I believe the family still own that smallholding today. In fact John actually tried to turn it into a working farm. He bought a tractor and planted grass, as he told Letterman, "I actually bought a tractor this summer, an old 1947 Massey Harris, and er the lines aren't exactly equal, it was my first time, I ploughed the field." Letterman asks, "What will you plant?", John replies "Just grass. Just grass, I don't want to push it, I don't want to push it."

In fact later on that smallholding the family would try and farm beef cattle, after the first few went to the slaughterhouse they didn't eat meat for a while and the rest became pets. There is a story John tells where the cows actually got out of their field and he had to round them up in his golf cart. That in itself must have been comedy gold. There were also horses rescued, in John's words "saved from the glue factory", ducks that unfortunately the fox fancied, a few cats and a dog called Keema.

Aside from the initial (rather large) teething problems, that property actually sounds like heaven.

Big City Comedy

In 1980 at the end of *SCTV* Season 2, John, Catherine O'Hara and Harold Ramis left. They were replaced by Tony Rosato, Robin Duke and Rick Moranis for Season 3 which was filmed in Edmonton, Alberta.

Greg Stillwell and his friend Bill were huge *SCTV* fans. One day, whilst sitting around at home, they flicked through the phone book and found an entry for a 'J F Candy'.

Stillwell told me, "We thought, could that be him? I was a little nervous. I said 'Give him a call Bill, give him a call'. So he did. I went into the bedroom on another phone so all three of us were on the line. Bill and John did most of the talking, and John Candy was amazing, he was just so friendly. We told him how much we loved him and he was very thankful and he said 'Hey! Do you guys wanna meet for lunch?' We went Downtown Toronto, he had an office on Prince Arthur Avenue, in what was previously a living room of a big house. There was a big long wooden meeting table, we went in there and I was a nervous wreck. But he was so warm and relaxed, he sat at the end of the table with his back to the living room window. At the time I used to smoke cigarettes, so we all lit up, I was getting a light from Bill and my hand was shaking like a leaf. Within seconds he was talking about his career and things that were going on with him at that time and within 15 minutes I felt like I'd known him forever. We must have sat there for an hour and a half.

"He had just left *SCTV* at that time. He talked about *1941*, the movie with Dan (Aykroyd). He said it was slow moving but it was a beginning, a start, not the biggest part but something. He told us to call and we'd have lunch again, he let us come and see him at the office many times."

After John moved offices Stillwell didn't see him for a while, luckily tickets to John's new show *Big City Comedy* were free and they got to reconnect.

Big City Comedy was a break out vehicle for John, he wanted his own show where he was the host. Picked up by CTV, John had a team of comedians working with him on *Big City Comedy*, including regulars Tino Insana, Tim Kazurinsky, Don Lamont, Audrie Neean and Patti Oatman. On the writing side John was working with Michael Short (Martin's brother), Jim Staahl and Jim Fisher.

Tim Kazurinsky met John after co-writing the pilot for *Big City Comedy*, Kazurinsky told me, "The show was to be shot in Canada and they needed some American talent in the cast so I was one of the lucky Yanks.

"We shot the pilot at the Osmonds' studio in Orem, Utah. John was brilliant. His energy carried us through. He was not just the star of the show, he was head cheerleader as well as chief cook and bottle-washer. I was in awe of his magnetism and his energy.

"We were deep into Mormon country… a place where the Latter Day Saints folk consider it a sin to partake of caffeine, nicotine and alcohol. After a couple of tense days, John went to Merle Osmond, I believe it was Merle… so many Osmonds…, and told him that if we were not provided with a coffee machine, some ash trays, and the address of some place we could get beer — the pilot would never get finished!

"John got it all… immediately. And we had a blast making that pilot. The wonderful and brilliant Ann Ryerson did the pilot with us but did not do the series because of her pregnancy.

"Guest hosts included Betty White, Fred Willard, McLean Stevenson, Billy Crystal, and Rita Moreno — who was wonderful — but slapped me every time I cursed. And the crew were the best. Especially Juul Haalmeyer and his mom (Trudy)[1], just hilarious,

---

[1] Juul told me, "My mother was inconsolable after dad died and I was afraid to leave her alone, and had to go to Montreal to do two series. So I made her quit her job at the bank, made it very clear she'd never work as a registered nurse again, and that she'd really enjoy working 18 hours a day, seven days a week, and we both got on the plane. The rest is history; she was the best assistant I ever had, but it meant we lived together, worked

lovely folk. Not for a single minute did it seem like work. It was more like a paid vacation."

In theory the show should have been a smash hit, unfortunately though it never really took off and was cancelled after one season. This was no fault of John's or the other cast members, due to the time of day the show was aired in the US it needed to be a family friendly show and gave very little control to John, he just couldn't make the show what he wanted it to be.

Juul Haalmeyer had previously worked with John and was thrilled to be assigned to *Big City Comedy*. "John was just always one big hug, that is the way I think of John, one big hug. He was always so up and so lovely and since the day I met him when he was very young, he was always just a beautiful person.

"I met him first on *The David Steinberg Show* when I really didn't know my ass from my elbow as I had never really done costume design, but they put up with me and they were very tolerant of me, including John, whatever I put him in he was fine with it, so I was like ok, I have got a career going here. No one slapped me around.

---

together, and travelled together, and that's a whole other story for my book."

"John was always so good, when we were doing *Big City Comedy* he knew I could sing, but I couldn't act for a piece of shit. He wanted me to do a couple of openings for the show where he wanted me to sing. I have a very wide vocal range even though I have never had any training and he said why don't you do the opening bit, with a grand piano and a high falsetto, so I did, and he said 'just fall off the piano stool at the end'. It was his way of including me in the show which was great."

Haalmeyer remembered, "John agreed to host the wrap party for *Big City Comedy* at his farm in Queensville. He invited all 88 people or however many it was to his house. So I called him the day before and I said 'John are you really prepared to cater for 88 people at your house?' and he said, 'I have so many freezers full of chicken and steaks', and I said 'OK and what else?', 'Oh I never even thought of that.' He said 'you're coming tomorrow right? Can you pick up all the romaine lettuce you can find so we can have caesar salad, and anything else that goes with a caesar?' I said 'OK'. Then I called him back shortly after and I said, 'What are you going to drink if you are going to have a party?', he replied 'Well I have got lots of wine and beer here', I said 'And? Do you have lots of glasses to serve the wine in and do you have knives and forks?' And he says 'No Juul, but you live around the corner from that party store in Summerhill right? Could you pick me up plates, plastic glasses, knives and forks and stuff', 'Yeah sure'. We got to John's house and with the amount of lettuce I had bought, his mother and I started washing the lettuce in the bathtub because it was such a huge amount, it was ridiculous. We ended up having to put it in bin bags with the salad dressing just to toss it all together. It was like John, yes this is you, big and over the top, lovely, well intentioned, not too well thought out. He was just so honest, it was exactly the way he was. You didn't have to worry about those details as long as the intention was good – which it always was."

Everyone at that party had such a good time they had to all sleep over. Haalmeyer had an idea to house them all in the large barns outside - however when he checked, they were full of cars John was collecting. So everyone slept where they could find floor space. Oh how I would have loved to have been at that party.

After *Big City Comedy*, Kazurinsky and John stayed good friends. Kazurinsky remembers, "One of my favorite memories of John occurred when I was visiting him on the set of a film in Los Angeles. While I was there, the big-time Hollywood director of the film publicly abused a crew member who had made a mistake... really tore him a new asshole in front of everybody.

"Afterwards, I saw John walk over to the director and I eaves-dropped while John, quietly but firmly, told the director that he never wanted to see any public humiliation like that happen EVER again. John said, 'You will speak to every member of this crew the same way you speak to me. With respect. And if you don't, I will walk off this set.'

 "How many times had I ever seen something like that? How about 'never'.

"What does that tell you about the kind of human being John Candy was?"

As *Big City Comedy* didn't last a season, John went back to *SCTV*, as did O'Hara to do Season 4, whilst Duke and Rosato went to *SNL*. *SCTV* had been off the air for a year but was finally picked up by NBC. However there was a catch, NBC wanted a 90-minute programme to fill their Friday night slot, so *SCTV* was now called *SCTV Network 90*. They were still filming in Edmonton and basically the group were having to come up with material and film 90 minutes worth every week. Juul Haalmeyer, their costume designer, remembers, "The whole experience of working on *SCTV* was the highlight of my life. Being around all of those wonderful people for that length of time, and it was especially terrific having worked with John on so many projects before that, but it just came to fruition on *SCTV*, all of those people together at the same time and having the privilege to be in the same environment as they were – it was magical. It was exhausting because we were working over 110 hours a week, but it didn't matter. I wouldn't have done it for anybody else but that group of people."

By Season 4, filming had moved back to Toronto and Martin Short joined them, although part way through O'Hara, Thomas and Moranis would leave. John loved *SCTV* but by the end of Season 5 he felt like he had gone stagnant. In interviews he spoke many times about how he didn't feel like he had much left to offer as he had been doing it so long. Once *SCTV* turned in *SCTV Network 90* - that was 90 minutes of comedy a week they were having to write and film, which basically equates to a film a week, that was very hard to sustain long term. It was time for him to move on.

Stripes

"My name is Dewey Oxburger, my friends call me Ox. You might have noticed I've ah, I've got a slight weight problem, yeah I do, yeah I do. I went to this doctor, he told me I swallow a lot of aggression, along with a lot of pizzas (laughter). I'm basically a shy person, I'm a shy guy and he suggested taking one of these aggression training courses, ya know those aggression training courses like EST and those kind of things, anyway it cost 400 bucks! 400 bucks to join this thing. Well I, I didn't have the money and I thought to myself, join the army! It's free! So I figured while I'm here I will lose a few pounds, and you got what, a six to eight week training programme here? A real tough one? Which is perfect for me. I'm going to walk out of here, a lean, mean, fighting machine." John Candy, Stripes

Greg Stillwell was in John Candy's office when the *Stripes* script came in, John opened it up, flicked through and remarked "Well I'm getting nearer to the front", meaning the parts he was being offered were getting a little bigger.

Released in 1981 *Stripes* was actually in the top five grossing movies that year. *Raiders of the Lost Ark* was at number one and *Superman 2* at number three! A military comedy with Bill Murray and Harold Ramis playing the lead roles, produced by Ivan Reitman and Daniel Goldberg, directed by Reitman.

The movie starts by focusing on Murray's character John Winger, who within a matter of hours loses his taxi driving job, his girlfriend and his apartment and manages to convince his best friend Russell Ziskey (Ramis) to join up for the Army with him.

Conrad Dunn, who played Francis 'Psycho' Soyer, shared his memories with me. Dunn had never met any of the cast before, however because of Second City, Murray, Ramis, Reitman and Candy all knew each other so he described there being a bit of an "inner circle", and John in general was "very jovial".

Half the movie was shot in Kentucky and the other half in Los Angeles. In Kentucky most of the cast stayed in a small hotel, the Ramada Inn, in a little place called Elizabethtown. However because John was married and had baby Jennifer, John was put up in a small house so Rose and Jennifer could be with him.

The scene where the new army recruits introduce themselves (see John's quote at the beginning of this chapter) was filmed over an entire day, so Dunn told me that they had a lot of time hanging around in that room and there was time in between setups to chat to everybody.

Dunn reminisced about going over to John's accommodation, "I do recall there was a big fight and everybody wanted to see it, Roberto Duran and Sugar Ray Leonard, and so John was nice enough to invite all the guys over to his house and his wife was lovely, she made a spaghetti and meatball dinner for everybody and we watched the fight. He was fun, welcoming, his wife put on a really nice spread. It helped with the movie as people got to know each other and have a good time, people bonded."

This was something John would do a lot, hang out with other cast and crew members, throw a party. As a rule it was probably just John being his sweet self, but actually it was also very clever, as people would gel together, get to know each other and that would always translate onto the screen.

One of the classic scenes in *Stripes* is where the troop are hanging out in a bar and Winger (Murray's character) convinces Ox (Candy's character) that he should go into a mud-wrestling ring with a group of ladies. John was actually very unhappy about doing this scene for several reasons.

Dunn said "I think he was a little ill at ease having to wrestle with a woman, I think he was of a generation where you treat women with respect and you certainly don't knock them around and throw them around so he was uncomfortable and ill at ease."

John was so respectful of women it would have no doubt felt unnatural and dishonourable having to film this scene, but Dave Thomas also helped me understand the other reasons why John would also be apprehensive.

"I was in the cast in the mud wrestling scene in *Stripes*. John was terribly humiliated by that fat joke, a big fat guy rolling around in the mud, Ivan Reitman making John do a fat joke. And John hated fat jokes and he wore a shirt because he didn't want to take his shirt off. People who exploited him as a fat guy kind of pissed him off, Danny (Aykroyd) didn't exploit him as a fat guy, he wanted him as a parole officer in *Blues Brothers*. Ivan (Reitman) and Harold (Ramis) exploited John. John was good natured if you treated him as a guy who was more than just a fat guy, he would let you get away with a fat joke because he was fair."

For that mud-wrestling scene the pressure was on even more so as a lot of the guys from Second City and *Saturday Night Live* had heard that there were going to be scantily clad women wrestling in mud so they all turned up to watch!

Dunn remembers "That scene took a couple of days because there was other shenanigans going on in the club alongside the mud-wrestling, the mud-wrestling was in its own way complicated, you had the mud and you had to keep the mud a certain consistency, so any time you have a lot of people on a set it takes time", and of course each time they wanted to start from the top Candy would have had to shower and get a clothes change.

Dunn reminisced about the *Do Wah Diddy* scene, where the troops are coming to grips with marching in time and the lead characters break out into the song, *Do Wah Diddy* by Manfred Mann. "It's funny, John and I were older than most of the guys. Most of the guys in the parading troupe were in their mid twenties and John was around my age and I was 30, so we were old enough to remember the song, I am sure Murray would have known it too but because he was the star of the film he was busy doing other things. It was funny because to both of us, we couldn't believe it initially that they didn't know it, we thought they were pulling our leg, but it was just before their time. We were teenagers when that song came out. Luckily it's a very simple song and very repetitive and also a form of the song is call and response so you can say a line and repeat it, we got through it. What was really impressive of the guys was the parade and marching around and handling of the rifles, we worked on that for a good week to get that down. It was very difficult to accomplish, even the people in the stands were local Kentuckians they weren't professional actors and they thought that we weren't actors, they thought they had actually brought people in from service to do the rifle drill because it went so well. Virtually anytime we weren't on the set shooting we were in the barracks working on that thing.

"It was fun watching them work, I didn't really come from an improvisational background so I was interested in watching that and it was fun to watch them interact and play together."

John's Canadian agent, Catherine McCartney, remembers that when the film came out, she took John along to watch it at the cinema. "When they were showing it up in Toronto I went with him to see it, he waited till the film had started and he snuck into the back, he said 'I just want to know how Toronto would act because it is home'. There is a scene where he is first seen on camera, and the crowds were conservative in those days, but everyone just burst into applause and John just had to leave, he was so choked up. I think he realised they accepted him. He was always on the quest for better and I think a lot of good artists do that, they are always searching to do better because acting is always about the next role, the challenge."

By this time Rob Salem was progressing in his journalism career, his first paid magazine gig was actually to spend the day with John and interview him about *Stripes*.

Salem remembers, "The first magazine article I was ever assigned was to spend the day with John. Two reasons why I don't have that article, one is John liked to drink rum and coke, the problem with John is you couldn't say no. He was always the guy at the party saying 'c'mon just one more' and you would have to. I spent the day with him at his house and we walked around his town and everyone of course knew him and we were drinking like fish. We went back to his house and he cooked something, I honestly can't remember what it was, but I do remember at the end of the evening vomiting my bodyweight into the gutter outside John's house. We were just hammered. Then when I did actually get down to writing the story, the magazine which was *Toronto Life*, decided the story wasn't Canadian enough. John had just done *Stripes* and his career was on the rise but it was perceived as more of an American Phenomenon, of course that couldn't have been further from the truth seeing as John was the most Canadian booster of them all."

Although there was no doubt *Stripes* was John's biggest project that year, he also took part in a quirkier project. He played several characters in an adult animated sci-fi movie *Heavy Metal*.

1982 John was also in a short film called *It Came From Hollywood*, where he talked about his love for Ed Wood and was driven off set in a motorbike sidecar by Dan Aykroyd donning a bra. Gilda Radner and Cheech and Chong also featured in this celebration of B movie heroes.

Sadly on 5th March 1982 John's friend John Belushi was found dead at the Chateau Marmont Hotel in LA. He had died of an overdose at the age of 33. This news devastated John, he was so upset he was sent straight home from work. He didn't surface from his house for a full week. John was worried that this was the beginning of the end, that they had all been thinking they were untouchable and now they had all had the most horrible reality check.

Always Meet Your Heroes

Imagine being 12 years old again. You are set an assignment in your journalism course to interview someone. You are the biggest fan of John Candy and you think you'll try your luck. You write a letter, and you wait. Then, one day you get a phone call. That's exactly what happened to Scott Edgecombe.

"I have images and imaginings of the phone call but since it was almost thirty years ago I'm not always sure how much of those memories have been internally embellished with time...and fantasy.

"I remember returning to our home in Oakville from school and my mom telling me that a man named John had called. My heart completely leapt out of my chest and I quickly asked her what he had said. My mother just replied, "I don't know, I'm not your secretary. And who is this man to be calling you anyways?"

"Since this was 1983, an eighth grade kid getting a phone call from a strange adult was mostly unheard of, unless it was the police or a coach of some kind and you were usually in trouble in both cases. I can't remember how long I had to wait to call him back but I was more nervous than I had ever been when the time came...

"To this day I swear he was totally playing with me because when I called and asked for Mr Candy (in the deepest pretend adult voice I could muster) it sounded exactly like him on the other end but whomever I spoke to said, "Just a second, I will get him for you." And then the exact voice came back on the phone saying, "Hi, this is John."

"Even as I type now I remember shaking and hoping I was going to say the perfect things to get my *SCTV/Stripes* mega-hero to agree to let me interview him. An important sidebar here is that the teacher in charge of this school assignment had been my nemesis since 6ᵗʰ grade. Getting this interview would easily make my decade.

"The phone call was quick as I felt I should say very little and listen respectfully but I remember him being very sincere and treating me like a professional journalist adult-type person.

> "Sure Scott, I'd love to let you interview me. Just give my agent a call and you and her can set it up from there."

"That was the bulk of the call or at least the part I remember. You have to realize that just speaking to him was like being sung to by a Siren for my eighth grade *SCTV* obsessed mind. I think he laughed once or twice and I couldn't move past the sound of his laughter to hear anything else. We all know that laugh and love it for all the places it takes us. I don't think I slept much that night. I wanted to call everyone I knew except the phone wasn't something that kids could freely used in our home so I didn't...

"But...I did get to sit in journalism class the next day and have my nemesis teacher ask me in front of everyone whom I had planned to interview for the project. When I said John Candy he blurted, 'You'll never get him', before moving on to the next student. It was another week before I got to tell him in front of the whole class that I had booked 'John Candy'. His face went blank and a little white as he softly replied, 'Oh'.

"It was the second most famous interview in our class. Ross Wace got Anne Murray.

(John was) "Larger than life and the pun is somewhat intended. Keeping in mind this took place before my 8th grade growth spurt and that just minutes before meeting John I was passed by Martin Short in the hallway whom at the time was still shorter than myself...

"John was a big man in both size and presence and he knew it because it seemed he made every effort to quell any inhibitions one might have upon meeting him. He may have been larger than life but he was soft in character and you could tell that he was completely there with the people he shared a room with. He asked about me, cared for how I was feeling and did everything possible to play down any idea that he was better than the next guy. He introduced me to everyone from the show whenever we walked past either a cast or crew member and was graciously attendant to every question or need I had and I'm pretty sure I was a rather demanding child. Most of my time was spent in awe of the mere fact I was not only sharing a space with Mr. John Candy but that he was escorting me around and treating me like an equal as we traveled through make-up, his dressing room, and some of the sets of *SCTV* circa 1983. The thing that sticks in my mind the most and seems to have been a constant in his life based on what I've read is that he always made sure the people around him felt important...I might even go as far as saying John's goal was to make those around him feel more important than others held him up to be.

"I will say that as we sat in the make-up room and I watched him being turned into the Mayor of Melonville next to Eugene Levy and Joe Flaherty there was adult room talking going on continuously. I had nothing of any substance to add but John did his best to keep me in the conversation and never allowed me feel like an outsider. On a side note, Joe was very friendly to me as well, but Eugene...well...lets just say he scared me a little."

Fast forward ten years...

"In December of 1993 I was living in Toronto and just beginning to professionally pursue an acting career. A classmate of mine from University who had heard my whole JC interview story called me up to say he was working crew on a one day charity shoot that John was doing for Famous Players theatres, something along the line of Variety Club I believe. My buddy said he could get me in as an extra for the day if I was interested and coming down to see John and hopefully talk to him. I jumped at the chance. But the really serendipitous part of the day involved a woman I had met the previous weekend at a bar up in central Ontario cottage country. You see, extras are wrangled like cattle on most sets, especially sets with celebrities on them so there is really never any opportunity to approach the really talent even when sharing an entire day with them. Well, luck or fate was on my side because the previous weekend I ended up in a conversation with a woman at a bar for at least an hour as she tried to avoid a drunk friend of mine that kept hitting on her. No numbers were exchanged as it was just one of those friendly slightly tipsy bar moments with zero sexual undertones. But…as I stood in my roped off extras holding area at the shoot the following week I noticed this same woman, Susan was her name I believe, standing next to John as he was escorted onto the set. When Susan's eyes wandered over to my cage I smiled and waved at her. She immediately smiled and walked on over. After a moment of small talk I asked her why she was here and she said she was John's assistant. Me being the slow idiot I usually am replied, "John who?"

"When she said John Candy I couldn't believe it and began to tell her all about the interview in 1983 and then reached into my pocket to show her the cassette tape of the interview I had brought to give to John. She smiled at me and asked me if I would like to meet him...again. Within minutes she lifted my wrangling rope barrier and walked me over to John who was still larger than life and fully bearded for his *Wagons East* shoot.

"John was kind and receptive immediately. After a few details he seemed to remember the interview but I was never fully sure if he was just being polite since that was his nature. We talked for a few minutes and I told him I was now 'in the business' which made him give me an 'Oh no' type response as he had tried to talk me out of acting so many years earlier. I gave him the cassette and found myself pretty much as flustered and nervous as I had been ten years ago. The shoot was beginning and John had already been more than polite to me so we shook hands, said goodbye, and I was escorted back to the extras holding. But before the day ended Susan made a point of promising me that she would make John listen to the cassette tape of our interview in the limo ride home that evening."

Making a Splash

"Sorry folks, park's closed. The moose out front should have told ya." 1983 saw the release of the much loved *National Lampoon's Vacation*, a film written by John Hughes (the first time John would work with Hughes - although they didn't really get to know each other at that stage), Chevy Chase took the lead as the head of the Griswold Family, on a disastrous family road trip, all to get to Walley World to make some family memories. On finally reaching Walley World, Russ Lasky, the security guard played by John comes out to tell the family that the park is closed. Griswold loses his patience and holds Lasky with a gun as they had just travelled 2460 miles and were not going to go home without some Walley World entertainment. Lasky then has to accompany them on rollercoaster rides until the police turn up. It was a small part, but brilliantly executed by John.

Going Berserk came out the same year, a film picked up by Universal, written by David Steinberg and Dana Olson, directed by Steinberg. John played one of the lead characters John Bourgignon, a limo driver marrying Nancy Reese, played by Alley Mills (*The Wonder Years*) and starring alongside his pals Joe Flaherty and Eugene Levy. Although it wasn't a great hit it kind of paved the way for what was to come. It was around this time that John first met Frankie Hernandez. Hernandez had been working in Hollywood and took a young John under his wing, he showed John how in Hollywood size meant something and before you knew it John was taken out of his Honey Wagon (a dressing room the size of a closet) and given a star's trailer. From this meeting onwards, Hernandez would be John's faithful companion throughout his career, although he was called John's driver, he wasn't, someone else did the driving, but Hernandez took care of John's every need.

Later that year, John got a call about a film called *Ghostbusters*, written by his Second City alumni Dan Aykroyd and Harold Ramis, and being directed by Ivan Reitman. The part was written specifically with John in mind, they wanted him to play Louis Tully, the nerdy accountant. Sadly, creative differences and negotiations kind of got in the way and John dipped out, the part, as you probably know, went to Rick Moranis, who John stated "did a great job". John was still in the music video for the *Ghostbusters* theme by Ray Parker Jr. You might think John had made a terrible mistake, however it was important he was true to himself, plus he had bigger fish to fry.

John's career picked up momentum in movie land, the critics really sat up when he co-starred alongside Tom Hanks, Daryl Hannah and Eugene Levy in *Splash*. It was Ron Howard's directing debut and the first film to be brought out on Touchstone - a subsidiary of Disney that allowed them to do more grown-up films. The film was a real collaborative effort, Ron

Howard was well known as playing Opie on the *Andy Griffith Show* as well as Richie Cunningham on *Happy Days*, so he was a director with an actor's soul. John could not believe he was working with 'Opie', Tom Hanks could not believe he was working with John and Eugene Levy, he was a huge fan of *SCTV* and had to stop himself "from foaming all over them", for Hanks this was his first movie role and he was taking the lead. Originally John wanted the role of Dr Walter Kornbluth, the crazy scientist, however Howard persuaded him he was ideal for the part of Freddie Bauer who was the older brother of Allen, played by Hanks. Maybe in the eyes of some this was an usual pairing for brothers but the chemistry and the polar opposites of character roles really complimented each other and were totally believable.

The premise of the story is that Allen falls in love with a mermaid called Madison (played by Hannah). When Allen was only 8 years old, he had fallen in the sea and was saved by a mermaid (a young Madison). Years later destiny brings them together again (although Allen is unaware they have met before), he falls in love, not realising that Madison is actually a mermaid, Dr Walter Kornbluth played by Levy seeks to out her secret. Levy was given the part after John suggested him for the role.

John played the womanising brother who had been married several times, liked to play hard and was basically Johnny La Rue but with heart. Although he didn't have many scenes, he made every moment on camera count, he had such a talent for enhancing every scene and bringing his character to life without detriment to his fellow actors, in fact he would always play the part to complement them.

There is one scene where Allen and Freddie are playing racquetball, Freddie has been playing for five minutes when he stops to have a smoke and a beer, he then goes on to tell Allen he's going to teach him a lesson in humility as he continues the game. Freddie (John) hits the racquetball and it rebounds off the wall and hits Freddie smack in the middle of his forehead. John was so happy that he managed to do that scene on just the third take. He said he smiled to himself, then he remembered he had to drop down to the floor else the scene could not be used, so he dived and it hurt, but he said it was worth it, "the crew applauded me and we went home early that day" he remembered in an interview.

Jill Jacobson was an extra in the movie, in the bar scene where Allen is extremely drunk, Freddie helps him fall off the bar, picks him up whilst hitting Allen's head and then chases after two beautiful ladies - Jacobson was one of them. The whole scene is perfect, it's only 3 minutes and 41 seconds long, however Jacobson told me that it took 14 hours to shoot, mainly because Howard was a perfectionist and wanted to get it just right. Jacobson originally thought John Candy was going to be completely different to the man she met, "I was quite surprised that he was the gentleman he was, I had a weird idea of him that he might have been a bit of a sleaze, but he was so not that, he couldn't have been kinder or sweeter. During breaks we would just hang out and talk. Tom Hanks at that stage was a tougher nut to crack, he was quite protective and not as open as John, but this was Tom's first movie. John was just so grateful for the work and to be there, I have met a lot of prima donnas in my time who would hold things up because they didn't want to do the scene again. John was just keen every time and happy to work over and over".

It was after *Splash* was released that John Candy's fame was cemented. Martyn Burke remembers, "He told me the story about when he realised he was famous. He said he was over in Amsterdam at the Anne Frank house, where Anne Frank lived before she was captured by the Nazis and he said everyone was staring at him, everybody was talking about him. He said that's where he realised he was famous, 'these people, these Dutch people, tourists who I had never seen before, all knew me. I realised that is when my life had changed.' And it did change."

Splash was one of the tenth highest grossing films of 1984 , making over US$69 million.

I'm still a Million Bucks Short...

One night Eugene Levy and John were in a hotel room watching late night TV, when a polka duo came on. They both found this really amusing, thought they looked like a couple of 'shmenges' (a mutual friend of theirs used to call everyone 'shmenge' and they thought it was a funny word) and a lightbulb went off in their heads. They wrote that night and The Shmenge Brothers were created. Yosh (John) and Stan (Levy) Shmenge, who were a polka duo from Leutonia - Yosh on Clarinet and Stan on the accordion, their band was called *The Happy Wanderers* and they had hits such as "Cabbage Roll and Coffee Polka". They forgot they had written these characters for around six months until they needed some material for *SCTV*. They also made a funny mockumentary about the band called *The Last Polka* that was aired on TV in 1984, filmed in just a week, many of the Second City alumni featured in it.

Also filmed in 1984 and released in 1985, Candy co-starred alongside influential and controversial comedian, Richard Pryor, in *Brewster's Millions*. This movie was the seventh time this story, originally written by George Barr McCutcheon in 1902, was adapted for the big screen. Herschel Weingrod and Timothy Harris, (both of whom worked on *Trading*

Places and *Kindergarten Cop*), wrote the screenplay and Walter Hill (*48 Hrs*) directed.

The story is about Montgomery (Monty) Brewster (played by Pryor), a happy go lucky bum, who has the chance to inherit a large sum of money from a distant relative. He is set a challenge to spend US$30 million in 30 days without telling anyone why, if he manages the challenge and is penniless with nothing 'just the clothes on his back' he inherits US$300 million. John plays Monty's best friend, Spike Nolan. They both play for the Hackensack Bulls, a minor league baseball team. Along the way Monty meets and falls in love with Angela Drake played by Lonette McKee, his straight laced accountant that berates his frivolous spending.

John wanted the part of Spike Nolan after hearing Richard Pryor was the lead and Walter Hill was directing. He went to see Hill on the set of *Streets of Fire*. Hill told John that he would love to have him in the picture as he was a huge fan of John's and *SCTV*, he said "I'm afraid the way the script stands there isn't much for you to do. But I'll do my best to expand the part for you."[2]

---

[2] On a personal note this was one of my introductions to both Candy and Prior. My brother, Dave, used to watch this film religiously. It didn't do as well as it should have at the box office, although it did turn a profit, and is often underrated by critics who assumed the film should be funnier considering the leads. For me it's a perfect Sunday afternoon feel good film – Tracey

Brewster's is also the first glimpse of a more svelte John, after he lost 60 pounds by spending a month at Pritikin's Longevity Centre in Santa Monica, laying off alcohol and red meat. He also went cycling every day. After the loss of John Belushi in 1982, which had a huge impact on John, he figured he needed to look after himself a little better and "get healthy".

It was also the first film Richard Pryor featured in since he had survived a horrific freebasing cocaine accident in 1980, where he was left with third degree burns over his torso and fighting for his life. Pryor had gone through a gruelling recovery, several times a day he was moved into a whirlpool bath where a mixture of hot water and antiseptic would be washed over his burnt body, his torso would be painted with silver sulfadiazine cream to ward off infection and he spent hours in a hyperbaric chamber – a vessel that would force oxygen into the body helping it to heal. On top of that he underwent surgery and was fighting a case of pneumonia. The doctors were also worried that the stress on his body might cause another heart attack following the one he had in 1977, so he was a true survivor in that sense.

Pryor has always reportedly been hard to work with, Gene Wilder had amazing chemistry on screen with Pryor but later stated in his book *Kiss Me Like a Stranger* that Pryor was easily offended even when none was meant, and that filming schedules were often done on Pryor's time, not anyone else's. Lorne Frohman, John's early writing partner, worked on *The Richard Pryor Show* just after *Brewster's Millions* and told me, "Richard was a tough guy to get along with, there was a big wall, I don't think anybody is going to argue that. The way you would penetrate a relationship with him was through good writing". However, Lonette McKee had worked with Pryor before on a film called *Which Way is Up*, so had known the comedian for a long time. McKee told me that John and Richard got on very well during filming, "Richard was always warm, kind and very friendly towards me and John" but she also acknowledged he had changed a little "I think because of his near-death experience in the fire, Richard had become somewhat withdrawn and reclusive; as anyone would after such a thing."

The first time McKee met John was during wardrobe fittings with Costume Designer, Marilyn Vance and Director, Walter Hill at Universal Studios. "What I noticed about John at first was that he was a very sharp dresser. Much like his character, 'Spike', in the film, he was snazzy. He was also very warm and engaging. I liked him immediately."

Filming started in Los Angeles in April '84, they had to finish on location in LA by the end of July so it they didn't interfere with the Summer Olympics. Location filming was concluded in New York City, wrapping in August. The Hackensack Bull scenes were actually filmed on a pitch called Bluebird Field in Sun Valley,

118

the field, which is no longer there, was originally built and used for a show called *Bay City Blues* that was based on a fictional minor league team by the same name, it was later used by local schools for their respective teams.

Princess Anne was touring the US whilst *Brewster's* was being filmed and was going to have a cameo in a scene with Richard Pryor, however the scene was filmed the day before she arrived. She was greeted and shown around by John and Joel Silver (one of the producers), they discussed many things including a recent fire that had broken out in Pinewood Studios, England.

Throughout filming John continued to follow the Pritikin diet and also had a treadmill in his mobile home, you could stop by and there would be all sorts of interesting people visiting him, frequent visitors included Eddie Murphy and Robin Williams. The hard part about a diet is not being tempted by anything else, although John was very focused at this time, he was still John, such a generous host would no doubt have a plethora of treats to offer any passing guest, everyone was made welcome and always felt valued in John's company.

There was plenty of laughter on set, a lot of retakes due to the cast corpsing, Walter Hill was very understanding and considered it part of working with two comedic geniuses. McKee commented that, "There was a lot of laughing and talking and interaction between John and Richard on set. I felt very close to both men and they clearly liked one another and enjoyed each other's company and humour."

McKee is an animal lover and activist and she discussed their mutual love of animals with John. Whilst filming was taking place at Universal Studios McKee wrote an irate and strongly worded letter to the management of the studios as she had heard they were putting tar traps in the parking lot to control the pigeons, "I got Richard and John to actually sign the letter before I sent it. Someone has to speak up for the misbegotten."

John would leave a lasting impression on McKee. "John exemplified a kind-hearted and gifted person with a magnanimous and generous spirit. I am forever grateful to have had the opportunity to work with such a genius and such a wonderful soul."

23rd September 1984 John's family was complete when his son, Christopher, was born. From watching interviews of John talking about his family I know he felt just so fortunate, they were the best thing that ever happened to him.

Summer Rental

In 1985 John received a phone call, he was asked to play the lead in a film called *Summer Rental*, the role was Jack Chester - a stressed out air traffic controller that was advised to take a break with his family. Comedy legend, Carl Reiner, had been approached to direct, he said he would do it if John played the lead, so they both agreed to do the project and John was thrilled to be working with such a king of comedy, saying, "I couldn't believe I was working with Alan Brady from *The Dick Van Dyke Show*". It was also John's first lead role.

Reiner told me, "I said 'I will do it, if he does it', I knew it needed a major comedy mind like that, otherwise it would not work. Even as small as it was, it was just a darling film to watch.

"I was waiting to do more movies with him, I said, 'Gee this is such a great experience, I have got to find something else for us to do' and I was actually looking for something else."
(By the way, Reiner was 92 when I interviewed him, his memory is just astounding! Far superior to mine and I'm less than half his age, just remarkable!).

Chester's wife, Sandy was played by Karen Austin, the children - Jennifer, Bobby and Laurie played by Kerri Green (who starred in *The Goonies* the same year), Joey Lawrence and Aubrey Jene respectively. Rip Torn also co-stars in the film as a Richard Scully, the rip off owner of a boat restaurant that eventually befriends Candy's character.

The movie was shot in St. Pete Beach, near St Petersburg, Florida and the whole thing was filmed and wrapped in less than 3 months! There was even budget left over - a complete rarity for Hollywood. The film for me was a strange one, the first time I watched it I found it a little disjointed, on second viewing I loved it, I have heard others say the same, you will find out why a little later on in this chapter.

Reiner said, "To direct, John was just a joy. Every day on the set we had so much fun. We had Rip Torn with us who was such a pain in the ass, we rallied against him, he was a funny pain in the ass. I remember at the wrap party Rip Torn had given us both so much trouble, he wanted a different boat to the boat that we had. But at the end he toasted John and myself and said he had never worked with nicer people and said to me 'I have never worked with a nicer director, I had a wonderful time on this picture' and I said, 'well I didn't as I had to direct Rip Torn!' John thought that was hysterical, he didn't think I would dare to say that."

Karen Austin, John's on screen wife, spoke to me about her time working with John;

"It was my first feature film experience it was the first time I was above the titles so I was very nervous. Although it was hard to stay nervous working with both John and Carl Reiner, both of whom seemed to make everything like play.

"The first time I met John was at the table read and we immediately entered into a conspiracy. We knew we were going to play husband and wife and we were just like 'oh I know you' as if we already had a secret joke, but I think he made most people feel like that."

Reiner cast Austin after seeing her in a play in Los Angeles, performing in front of sold-out audiences, Austin was playing an angry prostitute who was on trial for her sanity and bore no resemblance to the character he was casting. He obviously saw something in the actor and his instincts weren't wrong, Austin was perfect in this movie. Austin remembers, "So I do not know what had possessed him, but I was going through a rough time in my life and I get a call from Carl saying, 'Do you want to go to the beach with me and John Candy, a dog, a couple of kids and Richard Crenna?' Richard Crenna and I had worked before on other projects, one where I was trying to kill him and then we did this project where he was trying to kill me, so I was thrilled to see him! When I met John it just felt like it was going to be easy, and it was, everything about it was incredibly easy."

For Austin the three-month deadline didn't seem that intense as she had previously done a lot of television work, so the amount of time they had seemed quite luxurious. I guess the same could be said for John and Reiner with their TV backgrounds.

Austin remembers, "We did lots and lots of improv, because of John. We would turn up on set and John would say 'well how do we make this scene funny?' I would say 'here is some iced water you have to be able to do something with this', and he would make a whole scene out of it like it had become a thing."

One of my favourite scenes in *Summer Rental* was reminiscent of any child growing up in the 80s visiting a packed beach. John excelled in this scene, he was carrying the youngest child on his shoulders, trying to navigate a hot, packed beach, whilst looking for his family and carrying a cool box. In a hilariously relatable scene for any parent or child in that situation he stumbled onto people, the cool box leaking onto sunbathers and accidently putting out someone's barbeque. You could feel the stress and pressure he was under. It reminded me of awful beach holidays, where everything would go wrong but you'd go home thinking what a nice time you had - like your brain had a filter that only remembered the good bits. Reiner told me, "That was darling, he was one of these guys that if you set up the scene he didn't just give you what you had rehearsed but he would give you extra stuff. I was very careful to make sure I didn't lose any of his ad libs, going in that hot sand he was hysterical, I will always remember that scene on the beach it is one of those things you don't forget."

So why does the film feel disjointed? Originally John Larroquette's character, Don Moore, had a much larger role in the film. He was a romantic threat to John's character, Chester, whose wife was being wooed by Don. The film was written as if Sandy was going to run off with Don, and when shown to audiences at the test viewings they didn't like that storyline - so they had to cut it out. If you haven't seen the movie or didn't know that when you last viewed it go back and watch it, it all makes a little more sense when you know the context it was filmed under.

Austin's character, Sandy, loved taking pictures - in fact in the end credits most of the snapshots taken were by Austin herself. "I had not done any photography before and they gave me a really nice camera. So one of the things John did, he went to a bookstore quite early on in the shoot and he decided everybody needed a book. He bought everybody books and he brought me a bunch of photography books which I still have to this day."

John was happy to be working on the film, he was always extremely present. Both he and Reiner knew that the script wasn't as strong as it could be so they would both work on it or change the blocking (how actors should move to add dramatic effect, how the lighting should hit them etc.) Austin recalls, "Carl would just clear the set and we would work. I never got the feeling of we have to hurry up, it was just the feeling of we have to do this right. The only time we ever had to hurry was when we were losing the light. The hardest thing was on the boat, because how do you make a boat race exciting? Carl kept saying I need to get some tension into this. I think probably the most fun we had was painting the boat and restoring the boat because we got to do whatever we wanted to do.

"Carl and John had a great relationship, sometimes the two of them would compete to tell stories and you would paralysed with laughter, I couldn't get my breath I would be laughing so hard."

Reiner tried to look after John on set, but he did have concerns, "I really worried about was his health, he was overweight. I did something, I said John I am giving you a gift and I ordered a Pritikin menu from a very good health centre and we are going to get a Pritikin chef in St Petersburg. We can eat healthy and we will eat together and the temptation will go away. He was very happy to do this and we did it for weeks, but he could not help himself, after we said that is it for the day, there he was with a bucket of shrimp - we couldn't stop him and I had to say I have done my best."

John hadn't done a lot of love scenes, and there is one scene with Austin where John's character is so sunburnt his wife is rubbing aftersun on him. Austin remembers, "I don't think he had done a lot of love films with women and I think he was a little nervous about it. So I totally lost my nervousness about the scene because I wanted to take care of John and I must say I kissed a lot of men in my career and John was one of the easier ones to kiss, because I felt like he deserved it, he deserved to feel desirable and loved. That may have been our chemistry, I got delivered to him as a done deal, he never made me feel like he was unhappy with Carl's choice, he always made me feel like he was glad I was there. When someone gives you permission to be great then you rise to that. He was great with the kids, he was great with the dog. That dog had a pretty easy time of things, he was treated well. The dog felt very comfortable with John."

At the cast and crew screening of the movie Reiner gave a speech - not only did he mention how hard it was to work with Rip Torn but he also advised that they had shot a lot of footage, but due to the demands of the film some things had to be cut... "So I wanted to let you know that if some of your favourite scenes in the movie aren't there, or there are not as many scenes as you thought there would be, it is just because you weren't very good." There was also a blooper reel put together where the cast would be laughing so hard they would have to stop shooting.

Reiner's lasting impression of John, "Well, he was so in love with his wife and kids, it was just so sad he left when he did. And it was so sad, he was the most alive person I had ever met. In the movie, I haven't watched it for a while, but John would find these moments in the movie that could only be his, he was just that creative.

"He had everything to live for, he had no negatives, he was so in love with his wife."

Reiner left a lasting impression on John, in fact Reiner gave John the directing bug. Before working on Summer Rental John had no real desire to work as a director, after working with Reiner who gave him great lessons in directing and made him feel part of the directing process, it was then something he aspired to.

They had both agreed to work on a future project together but sadly that never came to fruition.

Fan Memory by Joe Kroger

It was Spring Break 1985 when I met John Candy. I was 16 and in St Petersburg, Florida with my parents and a few friends. Several groups of my friends and parents went to St Pete Beach every year for Spring

Break from my hometown of Troy, Ohio. It was nice to have friends with which to run wild on the beach and surrounding hotels, arcades, surf shops, record shops, and all the places teenagers are known to hang out. That year was no different. I had 3 friends that year to hang with. Early one evening, my friend Pete and I, and 2 sisters from Minnesota we had been chasing after, were walking down the beautiful white sand beaches of western Florida when we decided to go up to the Hilton and ride the glass elevator up to the restaurant for a nice view of the beach at dusk. We walked into the lobby and pressed the button. As we were waiting for the elevator to come, my buddy grabs me and says "I swear that desk clerk just said 'Sure, Mr Candy'", as he pointed over to the front desk 10 feet away. I believe I was saying 'No way', as I looked at the back of a linebacker sized man in a sport coat. The man turned around, and sure enough it was the actor John Candy.

Now let me pause here and say that I was, and still am a fan of Mr Candy. I was a massive fan of *National Lampoon's Vacation*, *Stripes*, and *SCTV* at the time, so to see him in person had me very excited. He walked right towards us, as we were between him and the sliding glass entry doors of the hotel. I took a deep breath and said 'Hi, Mr Candy?' He immediately stuck out his right paw to shake my hand and said 'Hi, call me John'. The other 3 in my party were also very excited as they shook his hand. I asked him what he was doing in St Petersburg and he explained that he was in town making a new film called 'Summer Rental', and having a great time with all the folks on spring vacation. He asked where we were from, then commented that he loved both states represented, and asked our names. We asked what he was up to that night and he said he was done filming for the day, and was headed to dinner. He had a car and driver waiting right out in front of the hotel. It was at this point I scrambled to the front desk in search of a pen and some paper so we could hopefully get a few autographs. The deck clerk chuckled as he supplied me with the requested items. I returned quickly to the group and listened as he talked about the fun of making *Stripes* with Bill Murray. I spoke up about how hilarious he was in *Vacation*, and that my brother and I were fans of *SCTV*. He talked about both of those projects for a few minutes, and then returned to the subject of his current project. I remember him relating the basic plot of *Summer Rental*, and telling us what other actors were in the film. I also remember I didn't really recognize any of the names. He assured us it was going well, he thought it would turn out to be a funny movie, and it would be out sometime that summer. I knew he would be getting antsy soon so I asked for the autograph he knew would be coming. On mine he wrote: 'Joe, thanks for watching *SCTV*, John Candy'. For my friend Pete he wrote: 'Pete, don't forget about that money you owe me'.

It was one of the coolest 15 minutes time periods of my young life, and it really stands out to this day. He was a super nice guy, very accommodating to a few young fans, and seemed incredibly down to earth. I remember watching all his movies faithfully after that meeting, and remained a loyal fan throughout his career. Years later, to my delight, I even earned the nickname Uncle Buck from my young nephews. It was a sad day indeed the day I learned of his passing. I've had many chance encounters with celebrities throughout my life, but my 15 minutes talking to John Candy stands out as one of the best.

He bid us farewell and headed off to dinner. We all rushed back to our hotel to excitedly brag at what the others had just missed out on clutching our autographs as proof. I still have that autograph to this day and count it as a prized possession. A memory of my brush with a great talent, a great guy, a larger than life movie star.

Gone Fishing

In 1986 John agreed to be part of a fishing pilot which was the brainchild of broadcaster, Terry David Mulligan. Mulligan met John very early on in John's career, when they both worked on an advert for Molson Golden Ale. They had kept in touch over the years and despite John's fame growing and growing, Mulligan had always found John very accessible. The show was Mulligan and an ex-Toronto Maple Leafs hockey player, Tiger Williams, taking celebrities out to fish. To Mulligan, interviewing John in a fishing boat made sense as, "What he (John) did best was play a fish out of water". Mulligan expands "I was good friends with Tiger Williams and I thought the two of them on a boat had infinite possibilities".

The show was called *Break Away – Outdoors with Terry and Tiger*. It was filmed at a fishing lodge in Campbell River, British Columbia, which is renowned for its salmon fishing. During the shoot, the crew played a joke on John where they filleted a salmon so it just had its head, tail and skeleton, fixed it to a rod and passed it to John so he thought he had caught something. As John reeled it in he laughed and said dryly, "Well ya know, I think there is some sort of pollution thing happening in the water here."

Of course whilst John was there he enjoyed himself, that night he and Williams went out on the town.

I was lucky enough to chat to Martin Anthony, a long time fan of John's, who met him that night and could fill me in on some of the shenanigans.

"I was living in Campbell River BC on Vancouver Island, working at a convenience store and I arranged to meet some co-workers after work at a place called the Anchor Inn. So I am sitting there waiting for my co-workers and they never did show up but I was sitting at the bar, the waitress walks by and I say to her, 'That person looks like John Candy!' and she says 'That is John Candy'. I said 'Oh my god I am a big fan, well do me huge favour, please take one of your gift cheques that you write your orders on and please get me an autograph', she said 'well I can ask him'.

"Five or ten minutes go by and I am trying not to stare at him and actually he came over and sat right next to me. He said, 'If you want my autograph you have to come up and get it yourself' and the waitress was there and she was laughing. I told him my name and introduced myself and he sat right down next to me. I was drinking a drink, I told him I was drinking Kahlua and milk which is kind of like White Russian but without the vodka. He gets up and he goes around the bar and grabs the biggest bottle of Kahlua they have got and about a gallon of milk from the fridge, he sat it right down in front of me and said 'Let me buy you a drink'. I was only 18 years old. He just started talking, I am from the United States, I have family in Campbell River and that's what I was doing there, he was up there filming a fishing show, I vaguely remember him mentioning that. He was with a hockey player called Tiger Williams, he (Williams) used to play for the Toronto Maple Leafs and was notorious for being rowdy. He liked to fight a lot, he wasn't there at the time. John asked me if I knew any old songs, I knew old country songs like Hank Williams and stuff like that so the next thing you know, I am getting really drunk on Kahlua and milk, we had finished off the whole bottle, we were singing these songs and just having a blast and people were singing along with us.

"The people he was doing the show came into the bar, the hockey player came straight in and wanted to fight with me, he just picked a fight and wanted to kick my ass, from what I understand the guy liked to fight, a lot. The waitress and bartender there were having a good time with him too, (someone was taking pictures but I have never found them). We were at that bar, it is more like a restaurant and it was about eleven o'clock, eleven thirty. So John Candy gets up and puts his credit card on the bar and says well alright, for everyone that is in here already this is now a private party, and he paid for everything.

"They eventually had to close. So we all jumped in a bunch of cabs and went to the other side of town to a place called Bobo's Cabaret and People's Cabaret and by the time we got there they were closing down too, it was about 1.30am in the morning, but they let us in. By this time I was having such a good time with those guys they thought I was part of the crew. So I asked him, 'why don't you give me a job?', and he said, 'well what can you do?' I said 'anything, I will do anything', John said 'well I will give you my number and I gotta go to Los Angeles to finish something, but I will hook you up when I get up to Los Angeles.' So I got his number, his autograph, the empty bottle of Kahlua, a picture Polaroid of all of us together and come morning time the sun is coming up, they need to go and do their fishing show and I took a cab home. I told the guy where I lived and passed out on the back seat, he got me home and I went to bed. I woke up in the morning and realised I had left everything in the back of that cab! We had a blast and that was it. All my friends about it were like 'yeah right!'.

"The hockey player did actually get into a fight with three or four guys and I am pretty sure he won. I was just at the bar with John singing songs and by the end of the night we were singing nursery rhymes."

Instead of going out with them, Mulligan actually went to bed early that night, but he was woken by Williams at around 4.30am as he recalls in his book *Mulligan's Stew*. "A hockey stick came through my open bedroom window and hooked me underneath my chin while I was dead asleep. It was Williams, hammered beyond belief. 'We got a problem, get up' he said.

"He and Candy had closed down all the bars in Campbell River the night before and had then woken up all the (fishing) guides in the guide shack and had gotten them drinking as well... Candy had passed out in the middle of all this, and now nobody could wake him up."

They were meant to be filming at 6am but they couldn't wake John until much later, John had to be back in New York later that day, so they fudged an ending, the pilot is actually available to watch on YouTube and is very entertaining, but sadly it didn't get picked up as a series.

Tom Tuttle from Tacoma

Volunteers was originally written in 1980, however the film was not made until 1985 and went through many changes, so many in fact that the only constant was a character called Tom Tuttle that John ended up playing.

Filmed in Tuxtepec, Oaxaca, Mexico, the crew built a whole Thai Village set, based on the Karen people of Burma's Golden Triangle.

John and Tom Hanks were reunited quickly after featuring in *Splash* together, this time playing very different roles. Hanks took the lead, playing Lawrence Bourne III, a rich kid that runs up gambling debts his father refuses to bail him out of. Being chased by angry creditors, Lawrence fleas the country by convincing his college friend to let him take his place on a Peace Corps trip to Thailand. This is where he meets John as Tom Tuttle from Tacoma (that is his full title), a graduate from Washington State University. They have gone to Thailand to help build a bridge for the local villagers, unbeknownst to them the bridge is coveted by a local communist force and a drug lord. There they meet Hanks' love interest (both on and off screen) Rita Wilson, who played Beth Wexler.

Ken Levine who was one of the writers told me, "We always pictured Tom Tuttle very differently from John Candy. We had always pictured a thin weasley guy to be Tom Tuttle. At the time we wrote it, Tom Hanks who really liked the script, was doing television and couldn't get many films. John Candy was off doing *SCTV* at the time and when Tom Hanks and John Candy got together on Splash and that became really kind of a break out movie, once we thought about asking Tom to do Volunteers, the thought was about re-joining him with John Candy. Putting them together for this. When the idea was run by me I thought that was not the way we conceived it but we love John Candy and he is really funny. I imagined the part would change considerably, but what the hell? How often do you have an opportunity to get somebody like John Candy to do your movie?

"Surprisingly he did not change a word of the script. He absolutely stayed with the script to the letter and yet made it his own and was absolutely hilarious in the movie, was way funnier than we perceived the character. At the time we wrote it back then for a Rick Moranis character. But John was just inspired casting."

Strangely enough Moranis and John were often landing roles that were meant for each other, physically they looked very different but in terms of building and living a character they were both just so versatile.

Levine remembers, "He was such a nice guy there were times that I talked to him, I am very much into baseball and John was a big fan of the Toronto Blue Jays, and so we would talk a lot of Toronto Blue Jays baseball. People in Hollywood talking about the Toronto Blue Jays? People in Hollywood have never even heard of the Toronto Blue Jays! It just made him that much more down to earth. I never got the sense that he took himself too seriously or his success that seriously, which is very difficult to do, because once you become A list actors Hollywood is just fawning all over you – all the agents, the PR people and the sycophants, everyone is telling you how brilliant you are. It's very difficult after hearing that for a number of years to not start saying, 'well enough people have said it so they must be right'. He was never affected by that, you just got the sense that he enjoyed the work."

The whole cast and crew got on great, it was a very light and fun set for all.

Even though the movie is over 30 years old it still gets regular television showings, in fact as Levine explained to me, Tom Tuttle from Tacoma is quite the icon in Washington.

"It's really fun, the Washington State football team still show the scenes of John singing their fight song during the games. A few years ago when Washington State got into the Rose Bowl on ESPN they were showing the crowd and the sports anchor said "Hey I think I have just seen Tom Tuttle from Tacoma". It's a character that has sort of taken on a life of its own and again that is all due to John and how well he played that character and how he turned the part into a beloved character. Way more people remember John Candy as Tom Tuttle in that movie than I think people remember Tom Hanks was Lawrence Bourne III, no one can tell you unless they are a real movie buff the name of the character Tom Hanks played. Everyone can tell you Tom Tuttle from Tacoma – like it is his full name."

Levine would have loved to have worked with John again, but alas, their paths did not cross.[3]

---

[3] Later on, after John had passed away, Levine campaigned to get John his star on the Hollywood Walk of Fame, something that has not yet happened and something I will campaign for once this book is out. I can't think of anyone more deserving of this accolade – Tracey

Armed and Dangerous

In 1984 John was asked to read a script, it was originally written for John Belushi and Dan Aykroyd in 1979, at one point Harold Ramis did a rewrite, then it evolved that John was going to do it with Dan and John Carpenter was going to direct. John had already signed the contract, written a cheque for a house he had secured near where the shoot was taking place, when he had a phone call that Aykroyd wasn't going to do it due to creative differences, which he accepted, then he gets the call that John Carpenter had also pulled out. John was like "well I'm still here, I'm ready to go to work" and Columbia said the whole shoot was off. A legal battle then followed, as Columbia claimed they weren't breaking contract, that it was "an act of God".

The film was about a cop that had been fired and a useless lawyer, they changed careers and became security guards, but actually ended up uncovering a corrupt union.

John was working with Eugene Levy on various other projects, he showed him the script and Levy liked it. They thought it could work if they swapped the parts around - originally Aykroyd was going to be playing the cop, Frank Dooley and John the Lawyer, Norman Cain, however John felt more suited to the cop role, and Levy the lawyer. So John rang Columbia and basically said, why don't we compromise as opposed to getting into a legal battle, would you consider me and Levy? They sent tapes of them both working together in *The Last Polka* and doing sketch work on *SCTV*, Columbia saw they had great chemistry together and agreed, they then got Mark L. Lester on board to direct and the shoot was back on.

Larry Hankin co-starred playing a stoned security guard, and remembers his time on set.

"*Armed and Dangerous* was the first time I met John. He knew about me, he knew me before I knew him. I guess he seen me on television or whatever, but he really befriended me. He was John Candy who I looked up to, as I was a big fan of his from *SCTV*. On *Armed and Dangerous* he looked out for me and he seemed to respect my work which was kind of cool. There was one incident where he stepped up for me, I put a funny joke in and the director didn't want me to do it, John thought it was pretty funny he and the cinematographer stood up for me. There was one scene where they were giving out the flashlight guns, we are all in a line, we were given a flashlight and my character in my mind was kind of doing Acid and stuff so when I was handed my flashlight, I immediately turned it on and looked into the light. I thought it was cute. So we did the first take, I was standing behind John so he didn't really know what I was doing so he got his flashlight and gun and would go, so at the end of that take the director said 'Cut'.

He came over to me and said, 'What the hell are you doing?' and I go, 'What do you mean?' He said, 'Looking into the flashlight, what are you doing?' He really had an attitude and was like what is this crazy? So I just said I thought it was funny, he said 'Well it's not funny, just get your flashlight and get out of there, let the next guy go up.' I said 'OK fine'. So I remembered John had turned around and laughed from behind the scenes when everyone else was giggling, we did take two and the cinematographer came over to me and said 'Why didn't you do that looking at the light again?' I said 'Well because the director said it wasn't funny'. The cinematographer called over John and said, 'John that was pretty funny wasn't it?' John said 'Yeah'. So they both went over to the director and said let's do it again but let's get Larry looking into the light, the director said 'Why?' And John and the cinematographer said because it is funny, he said 'It's not funny', so John said 'Well it is'.

It is such a small thing, but it was a major thing on the set. So the cinematographer asked for one more take as he just wanted to try something, the director agreed. So the cinematographer called the entire crew over, he asked them all to come to the set and just watch. So all the crew just surrounded us and he said,'OK run it again' and told me to do that thing again. So I did it. When it came to me looking at the flashlight the crew laughed out loud, so the cinematographer went over to the director and said 'See?', he said, 'OK fine' and since they had filmed that it stayed in. So John came over to me and said don't worry about it. I didn't really care, but that kind of bonded us, I would always check with John, 'Do you think this is funny?'

"When were we talking during the filming of that movie I would talk to him about writing stuff. So he would say, if you have got anything you want to write show it to me. I was writing film shorts at that time, he would say if you get something together let me see it and maybe we can put this together and make some film shorts. I really appreciated the nod from John who I was a big fan of. I thought, "If [he liked what I did then] it was kind of like a nice little nod, and gave me something to go on.

"I always liked him. He was the friendliest guy I have ever met, in the best way. He was really very helpful, he really respected who he was and helped other people.

"John directed me in the landfill scene, finding the comb, I found it and held it up and said to John 'Do you think this is funny?' I didn't trust the director and his humour anymore after that scene with the flashlight. Where I fell and disappeared down the garbage, John would laugh, so I would always check with John. The director was always asking me what I was doing and I would say I just thought it was funny, he would just walk away because he didn't want another scene on set with John and the cinematographer. He never got anything I did. By the end of the movie when they had the crew screening, the director came up to me and he said, 'I would like to apologise for the way I treated you on the movie', which was much later so I didn't even think about it. I hardly even remembered, but I said 'Why?' He said, 'Well I just thought they had hired somebody who was on Acid.' He thought I was that guy and he was afraid I would just freak out! Good job John was there to calm him down."

Steve Railsback did an iconic scene with John towards the end of the film, a chase scene, filmed on a bridge in Los Angeles with 200 extras, where John abandons his motorbike (which by the way he really couldn't ride, he tried really hard but was always wobbling all over the place) and jumps in Railsback The Cowboy's truck. Railsback remembers, "John had the biggest heart and was just such a giving man, which is so important to what the work was about. He was just such a giver. It was one of the happiest times in my life. From the very first moment, John was so gracious; he hugged me, a big bear hug.

"It's hard to explain but he had a gift, and his gift was life. He had so much fun, we would just improvise things, things would come up and he would just let me go with it.

He was a very special man and I just loved him very much. He had an incredible mind. There is so much I can say about John, I just loved being around him. That smile of his, that laugh of his, totally infectious.

"Many times couldn't make it through the scene because of laughing and banter, back and forth which is just so contagious, his mind was just born with this gift. You look at *Planes, Trains and Automobiles*, he would do so many different emotions, he would get you on so many depths, he was a great actor, he made you want to laugh and cry. I don't think there is anything John couldn't do.

"I can't remember how it came up but we started talking about things we were watching in our trailers and we talked about our favourite films. I can't remember who brought it up first but I was talking about my favourite film *Soldier in the Rain* with Steve McQueen and Jackie Gleason, a black and white film and that was his favourite film too! Paramount was the picture and he wanted to remake *Soldier in the Rain* and so did I, I was going to do Steve McQueen's part and he was going to do Jackie Gleason. It was a drama, god we loved that film.

"During that scene I said to him before hand, 'you don't care what I say to you do you?' He said 'no'. That's when I say in the film 'Jump up on here Slim', he laughed and it just took off from there."

On one of the takes where John was filming on the bridge he went to sit and wait in his trailer, everyone forgot to tell him they were going home. So they had cleared the whole bridge of 200 extras and John was still sitting patiently in his trailer. His driver, Frankie Hernandez, said to him, 'everyone has gone', John thought that was a joke and continued to sit there, as he recalled on a tv interview with David Letterman.

John added to his trusty team whilst on this film by hiring Bob Crane Jr to do some publicity. John and Crane had hit it off well at a previous meeting, and later John would employ Crane to be his personal assistant. John was building a trusted team around him, Hernandez would call them the "Chongos" which means "monkeys". Other members of the Chongos included Silvio Scarano as John's personal dresser, Ben Nye Jr for makeup and for a while, Dione Taylor for hair.

Later that year John would also do a cameo in *Little Shop of Horrors*, a musical film led by Rick Moranis about a giant man-eating plant, John played Wink Winklinson - the crrrraaazzzzzzzzyyyyyyyyyy radio show host.

John loved kids shows, of course he was originally doing a lot of children's entertainment and was pretty much a big kid himself. At the end of 1985 he briefly featured in the first ever *Sesame Street* movie, *Follow That Bird*, he was literally at the end, playing a state trooper arresting Sam and Sid Sleaze (Dave Thomas and Joe Flaherty) who had kidnapped Big Bird. That was kind of John's in on *Sesame Street*. Caroll Spinney (Bird Big and Oscar the Grouch himself) told me, "we were lucky on Sesame Street, we never really had to approach the big stars, they usually came to us, especially if they had kids and their kids wanted to see them on the programme". I imagine John adored being on set, he was childlike without being childish - he must have felt like a kid at Christmas.

In 1986 John had a days filming with Spinney in a scene between John's *SCTV* character, Yosh Shmenge, Oscar the Grouch and Oscar's pet worm Slimey. Slimey was learning clarinet by mail, but being the 100th customer Yosh turned up to give a personal lesson and a plaque from the Shemenge Musical Institute! Spinney remembers that John and the makeup department would move the fake mole around on his head, just ever so slightly. In fact one of the puppeteers kept his mole as a souvenir!

After shooting they all went to eat at a little Italian just over the road from the studio. Spinney remembers John ate spaghetti and meatballs and they chatted about all kinds of subjects, including John telling Spinney that he always thought he was going to die young.

Big Bear Chase Me

Imagine being chased.

Now imagine you are being chased through a wood.

It is raining heavily and you are trying to navigate your way through trees, over roots, through the terrain debris littered on the floor.

Imagine that the thing that is chasing you weighs over 800 pounds, has four legs, claws like razors, and a guttural roar that makes the ground beneath your feet shudder.

Your heart is pounding, it's leaping out of your chest and you can hear it thumping in your head.

You slip a little.

Looking over your shoulder you can see the beast advancing. Your brow covered with sweat. You are literally running for your life.

Anyone who put themselves in this situation on purpose would - have to be a little crazy, or very dedicated to their art.

That's exactly what John did, in one of the most memorable scenes in The Great Outdoors, *and he was terrified.*

Go south west of Yosemite National Park, California and it won't be long before you hit Bass Lake Lodge, a 1940s resort that was the location for another John Candy and John Hughes classic, *The Great Outdoors* filmed in 1987.

Director, Howard Deutch (who had previously worked for Hughes when he directed *Pretty In Pink*), had not met John prior to *The Great Outdoors*, which was originally going to be called *Big Country*. Hughes had convinced Deutch that he should direct the film. John was excited to play the part of Chester 'Chet' Ripley, a sweet family man wanting to take his wife and kids on a holiday that would get them back to nature. Stephanie Faracy played his wife, Connie, and Chris Young and Ian Giatti would play their sons, Buckley and Ben respectively. After reading the script John was convinced his character should have a beard covering his face, after Deutch discussed this with Universal, the feedback was "he can't have that beard, you can't see his face!" Hughes advised Deutch he would have to be the one to tell John the bad news, "Candy was really upset about it, 'this is my character and now this movie will always be a black spot on my soul'. He was pissed. We got off to a very rocky start because he was unhappy. However he never ever leaked that into his work, he never had an attitude, he was a fantastic person and one of my favourite people I have ever worked with. He was just an amazingly sweet man, the funniest, you can just imagine, but generous, generous, generous and always very giving to the other actors and me and everyone, but he was upset about the beard!"

The holiday for the Ripleys, although maybe a little more rustic than they remembered (Chet and Connie went there for their honeymoon), was going ok until out of the blue Connie's sister turns up with her arrogant investor husband and twin girls. So John is reunited with his old pal and Second City Alumni, Dan Aykroyd who plays his brother in law, Roman Craig, co-starring Annette Bening playing his wife, Kate, along with Hillary and Rebecca Gordon as their twin daughters, Cara and Mara - who to be fair, could give the Grady daughters in *The Shining* a run for their money. Aykroyd really pushed to get the part and Hughes was thrilled he wanted to be involved. According to Deutch, Candy, Hughes and Aykroyd were all very similar: "Candy was from Canada and John (Hughes) from Chicago but they were definitely kindred spirits and they both had this sense of blue collared glory to them, they adored Aykroyd – he wanted to be a cop. Those were their sort of people, they enjoyed smoking cigarettes and hanging out, it was everything to them, that is what they loved."

Dan and John (Candy) got on so well, they adored each other, you would think with their improv background they may have continually gone off script, however according to Deutch they were very professional and stuck to script as much as possible. In fact Aykroyd even helped with some of the rewrites for the third act which "needed some work".

Back to the film: For Chet this is his worst nightmare, he wanted a quiet family holiday which has now been gatecrashed by his arrogant and materialistic in-laws. Many hijinks ensue along the way, Chet accidently being dragged around the lake on water skis (he didn't even want to water ski, he wanted to rent a pontoon boat only to be berated by Roman), late night stories of a bald-headed bear (bald headed as Chet had come face to face with it on a previous visit, taken a shot and blown the hair off its head), an extremely persistent bat, pesky raccoons that seemed to torment Chet, meeting a host of crazy characters including 'Lightning Rod Reg' - a man that had been struck by lightning 66 times in the head! Not to mention conquering the old 96er, 'a 96-pound prime aged beef steak' that if ordered and consumed in its entirety (including the gristle and fat), the restaurant would grant your whole party a free bill.

As the story unfolds it turns out Roman made a bad investment, is totally broke and was hoping to hit Chet up for some money. The brother in laws never really got on; however on a stormy night when the twins go missing, the two are brought together through adversity.

The twins fall down a mineshaft and can't get out, Chet and Roman discover them, Chet encourages Roman to go down the hole to comfort his girls, whilst he goes to get some rope. Meanwhile, Roman finds out there is dynamite in the hole and manages to get the two girls out. Unbeknownst to Chet, he goes back, throws down the rope and much to his surprise helps the bald-headed bear out of the shaft, only to be chased through the woods by him.

The bear was played by Bart the Bear and John was terrified of him, however as Deutch explained to me they needed to work together, "There was one time when I had to do a shot where there was a bear in the shot (the big bear chase me lead up) and he (John), was afraid of the bears, but I had to get a shot of them both. I told him we need to do it but it will only take thirty seconds, he did it but he was mad at me. There was no CGI in those days, he had to do it for real." I bet John had never run so fast in his life! Of course Bart the Bear was well trained by Doug and Lynne Seus who have worked as animal trainers in Hollywood for years, they rescued Bart and his sister after the bear's mum was killed. I was hoping to get an interview with them about working with John, I was never able to but they did send me a statement saying that "John was so very kind to us, the lowly bear trainers in the 'prop department'. We can't say enough good words about him. A beautiful human being." That was typical of John, everyone on set loved him, he gave everyone the same amount of respect and love, he was always such a sweet Canadian boy at heart.

According to Deutch, it was obvious at times that John had some demons, although it never, ever affected his work, even if he had been up all night he would turn up on set with no sleep and work as hard as ever. "He ate, he drank, he would come back having not slept sometimes and that was not a secret. When my kids came to visit me once he said to them 'whatever you want come look in my fridge', he took them on to his trailer and he had like five lunches in there. But the thing is he never showed those demons, he was private about it, he never ever lost his temper, never ever was a diva – never! I don't care if he had been up for a week he would always be professional."

Joking around on set John was overheard saying he was in *Demolition Man* – the scene at Taco Bell 'I was in that', 'You were?' 'Yeah I was in the back, waving. *Gone With the Wind* – I was in that, I was in the side there.' A little kid came to visit the set and John told the child how amazing his life was "look I get to sing and dance and tell jokes and they pay me for it, what could be better than that?"

Deutch had convinced himself that the film was going to be a flop, "I was just absolutely paralysed and I went away with my girlfriend and I didn't pick up the phone, and then Monday morning it was a huge success and everyone was like calling me". In fact the film, released in 1988, grossed over US$41 million and is still a timeless favourite for Candy and Aykroyd fans. The lodge they actually filmed in was a replica from Lake Bass, it can still be seen to this day on the Universal Studios tour.

Howard Deutch told me how much Candy and Hughes loved each other, to the point where he thinks they fell in love with each other, total soul mates, "They should have been married, they would have been married had they have been gay". They would talk every night, they knew everything about each other, share stories, make up jokes, go out for the same kind of food. What also struck me was how Deutch told me Hughes didn't think he was going to be around for a long time, like he knew the clock was ticking, just like Candy did. "Candy made Hughes laugh and Hughes was a brilliant writer and once he got his kind of fangs into a person whether it was Molly (Ringwald) or Candy, then that personality would ignite him and he could write a character around that person. A figment of his mind of that character became a collision of the real person and the character; they shared responsibility of that, emerging out of a character he wrote that comes tailor-made, it fits like a glove."

They really were a marriage made in Hollywood heaven.

Above: Jim and John Candy circa 1955, photo courtesy of
Shawn Chaplin.

Below: John Candy and Jonathan O'Mara, Niagara Falls,
1969, copyright Jonathan O'Mara.

Above: What was The Donlands Theatre, copyright
Jonathan O' Mara 2015.
Below: Neil McNeil High School, copyright Jonathan
O'Mara 2015.

Above: Walter Olkewicz, John Candy and Mickey Rourke on the set of 1941 in 1979, copyright Walter Olkewicz 1979.

Below: John Candy's Star on the Canadian Walk of Fame, King Street West. John was inducted posthumously in 1998, copyright Tracey J Morgan 2018.

Above: John Candy and Rick Lazzarini on the set of Spaceballs, copyright Rick Lazzarini 1986.

Above: Dione Taylor (Hair stylist) with John Candy on the set of Spaceballs, copyright Rick Lazzarini 1986.

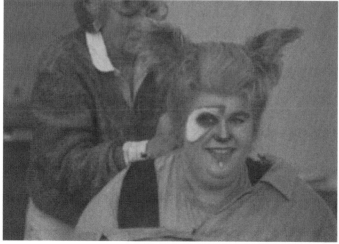

I like me…

John Hughes wrote a masterpiece in just over a weekend, 'masterpiece' being an understatement. A classic that everyone loves, gets played repeatedly every year - especially at American Thanksgiving. It shows the huge heart of strangers from worlds apart - coming together (even if one is reluctant). The acting and writing could not have been more perfect. Of course, I am talking about the great, *Planes, Trains and Automobiles* (*PTA*), with co-leads Steve Martin and John Candy acting their hearts out, making you laugh and cry with just the lift of an eyebrow.

As I mentioned before, Howard Deutch was going to direct *PTA*, but when they cast Martin and Candy together, John Hughes could not let the project go and decided he had to direct it and advised Deutch he could do *Big Country/The Great Outdoors* instead.

Neal Page (Martin), is the straight man, he has the well paid job as an advertising executive, which also brings the long commute, and he is desperately trying to get from New York City, to home in Chicago, to spend Thanksgiving with his beautiful wife and 2.4 kids. The weather and transport issues have other ideas. Neal encounters Del Griffith (Candy) enroute, who is a wandering Shower Curtain Salesman. Their first introduction was Del stealing Neal's taxi cab, (although Del proclaims it was a mistake) sets the tone for the initial unlikely friendship;

(The following is an excerpt from *Planes, Trains and Automobiles*)

Del: "I know you, don't I? I'm usually very good with names, but I'll be damned if I haven't

forgotten yours."

Neal: "You stole my cab."

Del: (Chuckling) "I've never stolen anything in my life!"

Neal: "I hailed a cab on Park Avenue this afternoon, and er, before I could get in it, you stole it."

Del: (Thinks) "You're the guy who tried to get my cab!I knew I knew you. Yeah. (Chuckling) You scared the bejesus out of me. (Pauses and thinks) Come to think of it, it was awful easy getting a cab during rush hour.

Neal: "Forget it."

Del: "I can't forget it. I am sorry. I had no idea that was your cab. Let me make it up to you somehow huh please? How about a nice hot dog and a beer?

Neal: "Uh, no, thanks."

Del: "Just a hot dog, then?"

Neal: "I'm kind of picky about what I eat."

Del: "Some coffee?"

Neal: "No."

Del: "Milk?"

Neal: "No."

Del: "Soda?"

Neal: "No."

Del: "Some tea?"

Neal: "No."

Del: "Lifesavers? Slurpee?"

Neal: "Sir, please."

Del: "Just let me know. I'm here." (Excitedly waving his finger) "I knew I knew you!"

As fate would have it, the couple are seated next to each other on the plane, Del attaches himself to Neil and aids him in his disastrous journey home when the flight is diverted due to bad weather. It is a beautiful comedy, full of heart. The film was shot in several locations, and due to the weather, the whole cast and crew had their own Planes, Trains and Automobiles experience - although as opposed to travelling home they trying to find the snow they so desperately needed for the picture (they ended up several weeks behind schedule and eventually shipped snow in to some of the locations).

If you can find the original *PTA* script (and it is out there in the ether), you can see how the characters are portrayed exactly as Hughes wanted, but both actors added a little something of themselves too. Hughes always encouraged his actors to improvise, in fact they would finish the scene and not hear the words 'cut' so they knew they had to keep going. If you read it you'll see where the actors went off script and just how much it added to the movie. They filmed up to 14 hours a day. Adlib after adlib, often in the freezing cold. Hughes had so much footage that the initial cut was four and a half hours long, I would have so loved to have seen that, a lot of comedy gold must have ended up on the cutting room floor. You can actually find one deleted scene on Youtube where Del and Neal are eating their in-flight dinners, it's hilarious, I have no idea why it was left out.

Candy really found his acting chops in this film, it's up there with some of his finest work and he never fails to make me laugh and cry, no matter how many times I have watched his performance.

Del's speech after Neal has laid into him at the hotel room was just magnificent, the hurt in Candy's eyes, the way he delivered his lines, "You wanna hurt me? Go right ahead if it makes you feel any better…" was worthy of an Oscar. If you aren't already completely in love with Candy, it's moments like this that make you fall for him. He gets you right in the heart, he hits you when you least expect it - and you can't fail but to connect with him, he bleeds humanity into his work. Of course Martin playing the straight guy was also genius. Martin later talked in interviews about their rapport, "At that point in my career, this was the direction I was headed for-more emotional roles. John Candy was one of the best acting partners I've ever worked with. We had great timing with each other".

Martin also told JC Corcoran in an interview that he thought *Planes, Trains and Automobiles* was some of Candy's finest work, "I saw him do scenes that aren't in the movie that were just breathtaking".

Martin remembers fondly "It was the first day of filming, he brought all this exercise equipment, jogging things, stationary bikes, weights and everything, and then never touched them!

"Well, he was a very sweet guy, very sweet and complicated. He was always friendly, always outgoing and funny, nice and polite, but I could tell he kind of had a little broken heart inside him", which was possibly one of the reasons he played Del so well.

Hughes' mind was always working, apparently the script was influenced by a disastrous journey he once had trying to get from New York to Chicago, but actually his trip lasted 5 days and he reached Chicago just as he was meant to be back in New York. Hughes filmed everything, even when they were not shooting properly they left the camera running between takes which resulted in them using twice as much film in the cameras than a normal movie shoot would use.

From all the extra footage Hughes filmed, a 10-minute short was also created, from the 'Doobie's Taxiola' scene. Larry Hankin who played Doobie told me:

"I revered John (Hughes), I was very happy to work with him, he made great movies and this guy knew 'funny'. He was watching me and John (Candy) hang out and riff, so John Hughes set aside a whole afternoon of me, John and Steve Martin to work in the cab. The cab was set up on rockers in a garage, we weren't really driving around. When we shot the scene in the cab, the actual scene you saw in the movie took an hour to shoot. But then he sent everybody home expect a very small crew, the cinematographer, the sound guy, him, Steve Martin, me and John.

"So for the rest of the afternoon we improvised in that cab for hours. It was really great because John and I were (from) Second City, so we were great at improvising, we were just playing together. We must have improvised for three hours just inside that cab. He (Hughes) was watching on the screen and he would come down and would just watch all three of us improvise and he would sit on this orange crate outside the cab, and he would say 'remember Steve when you said that? and Larry, you said that, and John you answer...', I was like this guy is incredible he has a photographic memory. So that was just really cool, I got to riff with two of the heaviest guys in comedy, for hours! None of that stuff ever appeared in the movie.

"A while later I was working with Chris Columbus on *She's Having a Baby* and I was talking about John with Chris Columbus and he said 'well yeah, I really respect your work Larry, especially that film short you did in the taxi cab.' I said 'what taxi cab?' He said 'you know that one with you, Steve Martin and John Candy, you were playing Doobie in that film short.' I said 'I didn't do any film short', he said 'well I was at John Hughes' house and when we were talking about doing this movie and he showed me the film short of you, Candy and Martin in the cab.' It was a ten minute film. So that is what John Hughes did with that afternoon of improvising. I have never seen it."

(FYI John also has a very short cameo in *She's Having a Baby*).

Other scenes that did not make the final movie included flashbacks to Del and his wife Marie (or as we find out later, his late wife), Marie was played by Susan Isaacs but sadly only the picture of Susan made the final film, oh how I would love to see those cuts. "To the wives!". Astute viewers may also wonder why part way through the film Del appears to have an unexplained black eye, this was also down to editing, Neal actually hits Del in the script, after Del admits he forgot to take out insurance on the hire car, just after it was destroyed beyond repair.

The wonderful "those aren't pillows scene" in the motel room was not in the original script, Candy had a similar experience with Jonathan O'Mara when they went to Buffalo as teenagers for John to apply for the Marines, O'Mara said it was so close to their experience "John must have influenced the scene". John remembered in interviews that this scene took forever to film, basically when the two leads had stopped corpsing the camera would then start to shake, it took forever for everyone to get through it. Another great scene was between Martin, Candy and Martin Ferrero who played the motel clerk at the El Rancho Motel, the couple stayed at. Neal and Del find the motel not long after their car had been on fire, Neal's credit cards were so melted they could not be used and Neal barters with the clerk to pay for his room with "$17 and a hell of a nice watch", Del's offer of "$2 and a Casio" were not accepted unsurprisingly! (You may also know Ferrero as the immoral lawyer from *Jurassic Park* that meets his untimely demise by being eaten by a T-Rex whilst he is sitting on the toilet). Ferrero was only on set for a day to film that scene and told me about meeting Candy;

"When I went on set that day, John was chatting with all the crew and he was on set practically all the time, talking to people and being very outgoing. He welcomed me in, he said 'I know we are working together'. Steve Martin wasn't on set a lot, he would do his part and then go back to his trailer.

"When I saw Steve and John work that day I noticed there was no improv at all, they didn't improvise, they stayed on the script and I asked him about it, John said "No we don't do a lot of improv because

John Hughes has written a script that is pretty tight and there is a rhythm to what he has written, if you were to begin to improvise you might waste a lot of time, it might be funny but you might be upsetting the rhythm, it's a heartfelt important movie and you need to stay on course."

I actually wonder if at this stage, because they were so far behind schedule whether they had also started to rein in the improv, I know at one point Candy and Martin had agreed not to improv too much anymore as Hughes loved them improvising, probably a little too much and they could do one scene fifty different ways.

Ferrero recalled, "John pulled me off to one side and said, 'are you preparing anything for your character?' and I said 'I have a backstory, but I won't use it if we aren't improvising'.

"I told John I had done a commercial for tacos where I had done my Jack Nicholson impression. So John said 'let's hear your Jack Nicholson impression' and I did it, and it cracked him up. He said 'You wanna try and sneak that in on a take?', I said 'I guess I could try' and he said, 'but you've got to mask it - don't make it too much like him else it will be just an impression - but the attitude was correct for the character and you should try that'. I said 'OK', on one of the takes I did try it, I snuck a little of it in at the beginning and that's the one John Hughes used. So it worked out really well.

"When they were wrapping up for the day, John said he was heading back to his trailer and he was going to watch the end of the Lakers Celtics game (the Los Angeles Lakers and the Boston Celtics), they were in the final playoffs and he said, 'Why don't you just come over to the trailer to watch it?', and I went over the trailer, he gave me something to eat, he would ask me questions about the Celtic and Lakers rivalry - he said he was really into hockey but he didn't know that much about basketball. I was very vocal throughout the game, John found it very amusing, it turned out to be one of the most important games in basketball history, it was the game where Magic Johnson took the hook over Kevin McHale in the last seven seconds, LA that night was ecstatic."

Greg Agalsoff was the boom operator on the movie and recalls, "I was certainly a fan of John's before we met and worked together. What made me a bigger fan was what I had heard of him by other crew members. Unlike other crew members who generally are introduced to the actors they will be working with on the first day of shooting, I was invited to have a beer with him in our hotel bar in Buffalo, NY, by John's driver and friend, Frank Hernandez. Several weeks earlier, when I ran into Frank on a studio lot and we both discovered that we would be working together, Frank told me that I would never work with a nicer person. He was more than right. When I met Frank and John in the bar, and was introduced, John was so very warm and unassuming. He smiled and said, "If Frankie says you're ok, then you're ok." A Buffalo Sabres hockey game was on the TV and I found out how rabid of a hockey fan John was!

"John got along with everyone. I mean everyone. He kept all of us 'in stitches' and both actors and crew alike adored him. John Hughes would have a most difficult time stifling his laughter in so many of the scenes that we did. Great to everyone, all the time, even   when   the   situation   was   difficult.

"A great memory of John was when the great Chicago Blackhawk hockey player, Bobby Hull (aka the "Golden Jet") came by to meet John at a bar location we were shooting in. John was like a little kid, meeting his hero."

One of the most heartbreaking scenes in the movie is towards the end, when Neal has left Del at the Chicago train station - they have done their final farewell and Neal is finally on his way home. Neal's first thoughts go to his family and the delicious dinner he will be home for, then replaying his trip in his head he laughs to himself as he remembers the journey, the adventures and troubles they had over the last few days, when all of sudden he realises by reading between the lines that something is not right. He makes a beautifully realistic link between his own family, Del and the conversations they have had about their wives, all of a sudden things don't make sense. Neal goes back to the station and finds a very forlorn Del sitting there. When Del is confronted he finally confesses to Neal that he doesn't have a home, that his wife has actually been dead for eight years.

Agalsoff recalls, "My favorite memory of John was the day we were shooting at a small train station in Pasadena. We had been doing comedy for three months, and suddenly he was called upon to do a poignant, heart wrenching scene. It was a side of him that I hadn't seen before, and I am tearing up when I think of the effort he put out (sic) and the incredible result we witnessed. When I saw the film, the edited version just didn't do to me what it did to all of us that day. John wanted so badly to get a juicy dramatic role. If I recall correctly, he went to do a reading for a very serious role, and was quite nervous about it. He was very disappointed when he didn't get the role (it went to Brian Dennehy). If memory serves me, I believe the director was Sidney Lumet.

"I didn't really hang out off set with John, but there was an occasion that stands out in my mind. While on location, he invited a large group of us over to his suite and made a huge pot of spaghetti and salad for everyone, with plenty of beer for all. We then watched a screening of a film that I believe he acted in, *Cannonball Run III*".

You cannot beat John Candy's hospitality, his ability to look after people and make them feel comfortable was consistent."

A slight but interesting tangent...

An incidental story I am going to tell you (but everything will become clear much later) is from when they were filming in St Louis, doing one of the airport scenes. So bear with me as this will make sense later...

Ken Tipton was the owner of six very successful video rental shops in St Louis at the time of filming. Now when video rental shops first came out, Hollywood didn't like the idea of them as they thought they would lose them money. Turns out Hollywood was wrong and back then, video rental ended up bring in more than three times the revenue of the movie theatres, so after a while Hollywood started to treat video rental shop owners very nicely. Tipton's distributor had mentioned to him that he was a friend of Hughes and that they were going to shooting a film called *Planes, Trains and Automobiles* nearby, he asked Tipton if he would like to run a competition for his staff where they could win places as extras on the movie. So in fact a lot of the people in the background in the scene where Martin comes

172

into the airport carpark and also in his "I want my fucking car" scene in Lambert Airport were many of Tipton's staff, of course Tipton also wanted in on the action.

"It was shot in the winter of 86, but we had some really weird weather that was messing things up on set. So the first Assistant Director (AD) came over with my distributor and I immediately hit him with 'I've been a fan of John's forever and I always wanted to be an actor'. I was a heavyset guy. I was really busting the chops of the first AD, he said, 'Well you are heavyset, you look a bit like John Candy's younger brother, how would you like to be John Candy's stand in?' I was like 'Hell yes!' I didn't know what it was but it sounded good to me.

"Basically what it is, all the snow you see in the scene is fake snow that they bought in - in a truck from Illinois where the snow hadn't melted yet. So basically they put this plastic tape on the ground, in the shape of a T it was called a marker. So I would stand there whilst they would set up the lights etc. in other words being a stand in is boring, you just stand there, but it's helpful that you look like the actor as they can get the right light, sound readings, sound checks, so 45 minutes of setting this stuff up, they drag me out of place, John comes out of his trailer, does four minutes of dialogue, cut, John would be back in his trailer, then they would put me back on the marker to film another cut. The only had two cameras, so they would shoot a long master, then a medium, then they would go for an over the shoulder shot. So basically 8 hours of me standing on a yellow marker and not getting to meet John at all which was really starting to piss me off.

"So at one point we did break for lunch or dinner, this time I could go eat in the big people's tent. I could see Steve Martin and Edie McClurg, but John wasn't there. So I see a production assistant, loading up a tray and this PA must have weighed about 90 pounds and there was no way that the amount of food on this tray could have been for this PA. I had the idea that maybe this was going to John. So I followed the PA and they started heading towards the big trailers and sure enough heading for John's. So I thought what the hell and I interrupted the PA and said, 'Hi I am Ken, I am John Candy's stand-in, John wants me to deliver his food for him' the PA doesn't know anything anyway, they are so low on the list, so if anyone tells them anything they'll do it. So the guy gives it to me and I ask which one is John's and he said 'the one that says John Candy'.

"I knocked on the door and I said 'Here's your lunch Mr Candy', and he said 'Oh come on in'. So I went in and I said 'This is a nice trailer, nice trailer', he was sitting over on the right hand side and there is a table and a couch area and he was looking over the script of what he was going to be doing later that day. So I set it all down and said 'Hi my name is Ken

Tipton', he says 'Hi', I say 'I'm your stand-in for today', and he says 'Oh, how are you liking it?', 'Oh yeah it's fine, but it's not what I thought it would be, I thought I would at least get to meet you at one time'. And you could tell at that point he was like 'Oh shit this guy's not going to leave is he?' So I don't remember what he said but it opened up to 'Oh yeah I'm from here and I'm an actor and do stand-up comedy and improv', then I slowly kind of sat myself down.

"Now I look back at it I realise what an asshole I was. This guy is a working actor, he's trying to learn his lines for his next scene and he has this doofus in front of him, yammering about this that and everything and I just sat there and rambled whilst he ate. And he's eating and looking at the script and he was so sweet to let me sit there and be a fool, it lasted a good twenty minutes if not longer. He finally put his script down and he's eating and he's looking at me and he says, 'Well you know Ken that's very interesting, you know what, you need to stop though, I get what you mean.' Then I said 'I've been an idiot I'm sorry', I have never been in this situation with one of your actual heroes sitting in front of you eating lunch and I tell him that what he does is what I would love to do. He said 'If you've got the passion, if you've got the passion for doing it you just have to follow it, but more importantly you need to realise that this is hard, it's not just fun, it's a lot of hard work, there is a craft to it. Just like there is a craft to be carpenters and plumbers and everything else, there is a craft to acting. It's not something you just do, you've got to train for it, you've got to rehearse, you've got to practice. People have no idea how much work actors do at home and behind the scenes before they actually stand in front of a camera and deliver some lines, and all the other technical things, how to hit their marks right, make sure the key light is hitting them properly, that you're not blocking other people and that you're not talking over people, and on top of all that you have to give a believable performance.'

"So he gave me this little pep talk about how it's not totally what people think it is and he was so nice about the way he let me down, not let me down but brought me down, 'Ya know what I totally understand you, everybody starts from some place, I was in the same position as you, I started in Toronto and did this and that and grew', and luckily he's now getting to do what he loves to do. So with that we left on very cool terms, I thanked him, he said, 'Ya know if you ever get serious about your acting and you're in Hollywood give me a call, I'll see what I can do to give you some advice, so you don't make all the mistakes I made'. I thought, wow, that was cool, and it was so genuine the way he did it, now in Hollywood people say give me a call but they don't want you to, they just want to get rid of you, but you could tell was actually genuine. I left there feeling good, I did my stand-in stuff and I didn't talk to him again that day. So at that point I didn't think I would I would ever become a professional actor, I was happy with my family in St Louis".

Hold on there readers, remember Ken Tipton, for we will come back to him later.

That Will Leave a Mark

Released in 1987, *Spaceballs* is a parody of *Star Wars*, and the brainchild of Mel Brooks. Brooks got permission for the go-ahead from George Lucas, "As long as they didn't make any *Spaceball* action figures", Lucas' main concern was it would affect the profits from *Star Wars* merchandising. John was cast as Barfolomew, a 'Mog' half man half dog "I'm my own best friend", based on *Star Wars*' Chewbacca. Alongside John co-starred Bill Pullman as Lone Starr (Han Solo/Luke Skywalker), Rick Moranis as Dark Helmet (Darth Vader), Daphne Zuniga as Princess Vespa (Princess Leia), Mel Brooks as President Skroob (an anagram of Brooks, the character is a version of Emperor Palpatine) and Yogurt (a skit of a merged Yoda and Obi Wan Kenobi) and both Lorene Yarnell (mime artist) and Joan Rivers (voice) as Dot Matrix (C3-PO).

The film was given mixed reviews at box office but has since become a world-loved cult classic.

Mel Brooks always saw John as Barf: "Nobody else could be that funny and quick". He gave Brooks a lot, including ad-libs, a couple were kept in the movie. "There was one ad-lib where they have a crash landing in the desert and he goes forward and back, and he says about his seat, 'Well that's gonna leave a mark!'. After I said cut he said 'I am sorry about that',

I said 'sorry about it? It's in the movie!' I left it in, it was beautiful.

 "I liked him a lot, he was an incredibly dear sweet guy and it was really an incredible tragedy for such a young, vital person like that to pass away. We liked him so much, my late wife and I would go out with him and his wife. One night we went out with them, we did a picnic basket at The Hollywood Bowl, a big outdoor event – equivalent in London would be Proms at the Palace, that kind of thing. We saw Pavarotti and John was so funny, Pavarotti had a big white handkerchief, and after he sang he mopped his brow with it, and he took a bow and waved this enormous white handkerchief in the wind, and Candy turned to me and said 'Oh look! He is surrendering'.

"He was quick and funny and it wasn't just using writer's words and free play jokes but his quick wit was always there and always ready. You never had to explain. There are few guys in my life that could do that, John Candy, Gene Wilder and Rick Moranis was very quick too. Guys like that I wouldn't have to write a script out I would just say 'this is what the scene is about'. It's called *commedia dell'arte*, it was used in the 16th and 17th Century. They didn't write out things completely, they just wrote the skeleton and the actors would add the feelings and the extra words and John could do that. I always said John you could do *commedia dell'arte*.

"That was *Spaceballs*. At that time I was really dead set on my own movie career and I was starting Brooks Films, with movies like the *Elephant Man* and *Frances*. So I was working 24 hours a day and I wasn't very social at that time. I had very little time so I couldn't go out for dinner with John, but he was adorably funny. We had a lot of laughs on set. Moranis would say to me 'What's the big guy doing?' I would say, 'God knows, go to his trailer and stop him from whatever he is doing'. He would be eating a turkey leg. From what I understand he was a very, very good husband. He didn't drink much, I poured some wine and I think he had a beer or coke, he didn't like wine. He was always a pleasure on set.

"I was kind of on his tail, I was kind of the food police for a while. I would go through his trailer I would search it for candy and stuff like that, sometimes I would find a great big Hershey bar and ham and I would get it out of there and he'd cry (Brooks joked). I made him vow, pledge, that he would not eat French fries and ya know drink beer or do anything that would put on extra weight."

Although Barf seemed to come naturally to John as a role, there was a lot of preparation to take place before a day's filming could commence. John had to go into make up for hours before he could do anything, Ben Nye Jr. who worked with John on a regular basis would do John's make up to transform him into Barf along with prosthetics makeup artist

Ken Diaz. There was also the case of the wonderful animatronic ears and tail John donned.

In steps the wonderfully talented Rick Lazzarini who worked on Spaceballs after being recommended by Diaz as he explained to me (there was no point to me breaking up this interview, I have left Lazzarini to tell the story)...

"My 'in' on *Spaceballs* was Ken Diaz. Ken Diaz was working as a Prosthetics Makeup Artist on the film, and we had previously worked together at BOSS Films, one of the leading FX houses at the time (*Ghostbusters, Die Hard, Multiplicity*), creating aliens and creatures there. I was one of the lead animatronics designers and creature puppeteers at BOSS, having previously been an Animatronics Supervisor over at Stan Winston Studios, where I had designed, created, and puppeteered the internal head animatronics and darting tongue of the Alien Queen, as well as the Running Facehugger, and the Opening Egg (from the movie *Aliens*).

"Ken said that he was working on this Mel Brooks film with John Candy, and that John's character, a Half-Man, Half-Dog, needed a pair of very expressive ears. I was excited at the chance to work with Ken again, and...Mel Brooks? John Candy? Sign me up!

"I was a HUUUUGE fan of John's. I love, love, LOVED *SCTV*, and there was a slight connection; he was lovable and funny as Wink Wilkinson in *Little Shop of*

Horrors, which was shooting at the same time as *Aliens*, at Pinewood Studios in England. So I would wander those sets, help out in the foam room occasionally during the making of the huge Audrey 2 puppet, and just felt a very thin, but very special connection to that project. And so, knowing all the brilliant characters he'd played, I had to try and not make a fool of myself by gushing all fan boyish when I met him. Which took considerable self-control!

"My first meeting with John, it was just great. Here is this larger than life guy, both in celebrity status and actual appearance, because he was tall, and big, but he was just so down-to-earth and friendly. His smile was so open, so beaming, so welcoming, you could not help but feel happy and tickled, just because he was there. "Whattya gonna do to me, Rick? They got this crazy makeup I gotta wear." I told him that I had two versions of the ears I was going to make, one where I would operate with cables, and one where I would operate them remotely. We eventually used the remote ears exclusively.

"So, Ben Nye Jr. and Ken were doing a makeup test on John, a toned-down one, as the previous version had covered up too much of John's face. As John put it: "Mel said: 'What's with all this rubbah? I can't see his face! What am I paying him a million dollars for? If you're gonna cover up his face, I might as well hire CHUCK MCCANN!" And John's chuckle, the way his eyes would almost tear up at that, was infectious.

"And so it got established that I would be in the makeup room with John, Ben, Ken, Dione Taylor, and Melanie Levitt, They would do his facial makeup and hair, he would don the ears, and then he'd get his hair coiffed and costume on.

"Oh, my God, working with John was like a dream. A happy, fun dream. I and everyone else in the world have had jobs where it's a chore and a drag to get there. Working with John, you looked forward to the day. It was like skipping to school. You got to work with this magnanimous, warm, funny, FUNNY man.

"One day, his Agent (or his Manager, or someone in a similar capacity) was going to come into the makeup room and meet with John. John said: "This guy, he's always so dapper. And he wears these super-expensive shoes! So I want you guys to find ways to like, step on his toes! It'll drive him CRAZY!" Okay! Sounds fun! So we did. This fella came in, very Hollywood, silk shirt, brusque, and very uninterested in the 'little people' there. Ken 'accidentally' stepped on his toes. 'Excuse me!', 'Sorry about that'. Then I stepped on his toes, a little later. 'Hey, watch it!' 'Pardon me, I apologize'. Then Ken found another opportunity to besmirch this guys' Tanino Crisci's, or whatever the hell they were. 'GOD DAMMIT!' The guy blew up. 'WHATS WITH EVERYBODY STEPPING ON MY FEET TODAY?!?' And John was CRYING. Bawling. LAUGHING in tears, his shoulders shaking.

You could see he enjoyed seeing this kind of pretentious guy taken down a few pegs.

"Then, another time, some Producers wanted to meet me. *Gorillas in the Mist* was in pre-production, and, as Hollywood types are wont to do, these guys wanted to 'hit the theaters earlier' with a competing film. But I was working, daily, on *Spaceballs*, so I asked Ben, and Ken, and especially John, for permission to have them meet me in the makeup room, where John and I both agreed might add a little 'BING!' and star-power to the presentation.

"Except, when they came in, they acted like John Candy wasn't even there. And they were…well, kinda sleazy. I wanted this big gorilla movie gig, so I was letting things slide. But John didn't like them, didn't like the way they were acting, didn't like their attitude. After one weird request from them, as I was trying to think of how to diplomatically respond, John said: 'You know what? Get the fuck out. Yeah, you guys. Get the hell out of here. Rick, you don't need these guys.' And so they slunk away.

"'I don't wanna ruin a gig for you, Rick', said John. 'But those guys are just no good. I can tell. You're better off without them'.

"And so, I appreciated that. he was looking out for me. He'd been screwed over by people before and didn't like to see it happen to someone else. And It just made me love him even more.

(In regards to controlling Barf's ears and how John liked to improvise)

"John did like to improvise, though he would give me notes, in some cases, as to something specific that he wanted. I was there to enhance his performance, and with his expressions, had movements, and ears, he could look: SURPRISED! Sorry..., Quizzical?!, and a great range of other emotions. He was easy to follow, and I'm quick on my feet, so I was usually free to go with it. Which never bothered John, he was always fine, but Mel... tee hee! "Enough with the ears, already! I don't need his ears upstaging him!!" And so I would have to sneak ear movements in, and John would egg me on, mischievously.

"But it wasn't always about the ears, and I would often just sit there, realizing: 'Oh, man. I am here, watching Mel Brooks laugh and give direction and bellow and joke, and here's John Candy, cracking jokes, adlibbing, being just warm and charming and...' Showbiz heaven, is what it was."

John was notorious for being generous and on the set of Spaceballs that was demonstrated often. He gave everyone on the crew a "Barf Award", which consisted of a golden dog bone, on a wooden plaque with the individuals name engraved on it.

Once John liked you he would be sure to develop a relationship off the set. He called Lazzarini up to see if he liked lobster as he had an excess of them at his home.

"So my wife, Deb and I drove out to his place in Mandeville Canyon. Rang the doorbell, and when the door opened, there's John, just beaming that awesome smile, just sending friendliness-and good-feeling rays straight to your heart and warming you up.

"A crate of lobsters was at his feet.
'Take as many as you want!' he cajoled, and we grabbed a few.

'Alright, you sure you got enough? No point in these things goin' bad!' And so, sure, a couple more.
'Thank you so much, John, this is so awesome!'
'No problem. Enjoy! See you Monday!'

And we floated away on a magic carpet of John Candy charm, goodness, and free lobsters."

John also called Lazzarini for help one Christmas. Lazzarini recalls the conversation;

"'So, Rick, you're good with mechanical stuff, right?'
'Yeah, I think so!'
'Well, can you come on over to my office? I need you to build something for me...'
With everything he had done for me, the answer was: 'Of course! No question.'

So I made my way to his Santa Monica office, where he greeted me warmly.

'I got this thing for my son Christopher. I dunno how to put it together!'

It was a metal tractor, the pedal kind, nicely crafted, solid, but it needed assembly.

'You got it!' I said, and immediately started on putting it together. It was for a Christmas present, and right around the holidays, and so John put on some Christmas music. He asked:

'Do you want some wine?'

'Sure!'

So we chatted, drinking wine, he behind his desk with his feet up on it, me sitting cross-legged on the floor, putting Tab A into Slot B and aligning holes so screw C could thread in.

'You smoke?'

'No, I don't really...'

But he didn't mean cigarettes. John brought out a nice looking joint and fired it up.

I thought , A: How cool is this guy? and B: Who am I to refuse his generous hospitality?

"And so...we talked, joked, laughed, sipped, dished, toked, mellowed, cozy, the red tractor coming into shape as we shared and joshed and enjoyed each other's company.

I haven't yet met another actor, much less a human being, with John's capacity to fill the people around him with such joy. God bless him. He was wonderful. I miss him so."

Playwright and author, Lisa Soland, got to spend a day on the set of *Spaceballs* and shared her memories with me;

"I had worked on a play with Ronny Graham, at the Burt Reynolds' Theatre in Jupiter Florida, called, *Arsenic and Old Lace*. The play starred Patrick Wayne and Alice Ghostley, Mary Wickes and myself. When I moved to Los Angeles, Ronny Graham, who helped to write many of the Mel Brooks projects, invited me onto the set of the film *Spaceballs*. I was only on the set for one day but I can tell you, I was so very impressed with Mr Candy. I met all the cast that day. They were shooting the scene where the alien pops out of John Hurt's stomach. Because the scene had many technical demands, most of the day was spent waiting around. Come lunchtime, Mel Brooks, John Candy, Ronny Graham and I, drove to what they call "dailies" together in this old-fashioned station wagon. We all entered the small viewing room and they played, for us all, about 20 takes shot from the day before. The takes were of John Candy dressed up in his costume, playing the role of "Barf," which involved his tail going up the waitresses' uniform.

"Take after take John provided spontaneous and unique responses with appropriate lines to match, each and every one different, for Mel Brooks to choose from. I'll tell you what, I would have hated to choose the best take out of those some-odd twenty. Each one represented a man (John Candy) who was hard working, innovative and brilliant. I learned a lot that day. New to living in Los Angeles and participating in the 'behind-the-camera' action, I was not aware of the true talent that Mr Candy processed. He was special and it's no wonder he worked so much and left us such a legacy of great work. He was well-liked behind the camera too, but I found him to be maybe more intense than most of us usually see him being on camera. He was funny off-camera, yes, but very focused. I got the impression that he was there to work, which impressed me even more."

Ear Candy

Catherine McCartney, John's Canadian agent told me, if you ever went to an event with John and he told you he wasn't staying long, you'd have to get him out of there before any live music started, as soon as a band started you lost him and he would be there until they finished.

John had always loved music, from playing the clarinet at school, booking the bands to play the school hall, flirting with the drums, helping book the bands that featured on *SCTV*, he couldn't help himself. From listening to Simon and Garfunkel as a teenager driving around on Friday nights, John loved all sorts of music, Dave Thomas told me he loved to especially play Eddie Money's *Baby Hold On* in the car. He also became friends with a lot of musicians, in fact fast forward a couple of years and he would have a cameo in The Travelling Wilburys' *Wilbury Twist* video - and it doesn't come much bigger than The Travelling Wilburys - a supergroup made up of Bob Dylan, George Harrison, Jeff Lynne, Roy Orbison and Tom Petty - for the love of everything good in this world! I can imagine John was honoured and over the freaking moon.

So with all this in mind, it wasn't really too much of a shock when John wanted to start his own radio show, *Radio Kandy* in 1988. He employed legendary producer Doug Thompson and built a recording studio at his Frostback Productions office. Frostback was something John had started a year or so earlier - it was basically a vehicle to give him some creative control back.

The idea behind *Radio Kandy* was that John had bought an incredibly powerful radio transmitter and he could take over the local radio stations' signal for two hours every weekend. It was actually picked by 350 stations over the States. He combined comedy with music, still developing some of his *SCTV* characters on air, having some Second City alumni to join him - regular contributors included Dave Thomas, Valri Bromfield, Joe Flaherty and Mike Short, they would even make skit adverts, just like they did on *SCTV*. Mixed with music John loved, he would also have musical guests including Peter Frampton, Phil Collins, Levon Helme and Clarence Clemons.

John would also go on to star in a Phil Collins TV special in 1990, *Seriously... Phil Collins*.

John told the *Toronto Star* in 1986 that he'd always had a passion for radio. "I never thought I'd be working as a disc jockey, but this show is so much more than that. I get to play with my *SCTV* characters, make up some new ones and have some real fun.

"The transition to radio is easy, as long as you concentrate on creating real characters. And the best part is I don't have to sit in the make-up department for three hours."

The show would last for two years, in 1989 it was even nominated for a *Billboard Magazine* Syndicated Special of the Year award, but sadly they had to stop broadcasting due to John's other work commitments.

Under Frostback Productions, he would also team up with DIC Animation City, Saban International Services and Worldvision Enterprises to make an animated children's series called *Camp Candy*. The comic version was also picked up by Marvel. The Camp leader was of course, John, and there was a host of regular characters Nurse Molly, and of course the children that attended *Camp Candy*. As per usual John brought his friends on board and worked with Valri Bromfield, Lewis Arquette, Danny Mann and Cree Summer.

Bromfield remembered a story John had told her whilst they were hanging out. "John told me a story once that I've never forgotten. We were talking about the ways in which we had been changed by the entertainment industry. He said being on a set turned him into a jerk. I couldn't imagine that. He said he came home from a 9 month shoot in which he was catered to and his every whim met. He said he was sitting in his living room reading a script and he wanted a soda so without looking up...or thinking apparently...he called to Rosemary whom he knew was in the kitchen at the time. 'Ro, get me a coke will you?' He said he went back to reading and then became aware that somebody was standing next to him. He looked up and there stood Rosemary with a curious look on her face - hands on hips. She asked, 'Did you just say something to me?' He realized in a flash that he had been a jerk and said 'Oh... no... no... I don't know what I was thinking...' He said he jumped up and went to get his own coke. I love that story. More than anybody I knew at the time he was that Canadian boy who was polite, and gracious and who considered the feelings of others. That's probably why this story stands out for me."

I love that story too, no matter how successful he was (the man even had his own cartoon!), Rose was his grounding when he needed it, she also bolstered him when needed. She was his ultimate guardian.

John also did character voice over work, playing the voice of Don the Horse in *Hot To Trot*. Working alongside Bobcat Goldthwait who was playing the lead, Fred Chaney, a bachelor that inherits a talking horse and part of an investment company from his late mother, luckily for him Don is able to give Chaney successful investment tips . Originally Joan Rivers had Goldthwait's role and Elliot Gould voiced 'Don' however it just didn't work and the producers recast. When John got involved he pretty much ignored the script and improvised. If you haven't see the film, think of an 80s *Mr Ed*, perfect viewing for any teen in the summer holidays. Sadly it was neither critically nor commercially successful, and was actually nominated for five Golden Raspberry Awards (aka the Razzies, a mock booby prize in recognition of the worst in film)!

Who's Harry Crumb?

1989 saw bumbling, endearing and slightly annoying, (that's some of the words you might use to describe) private detective, Harry Crumb. Crumb inherited his title via the family business, Crumb & Crumb, although he is well-meaning he doesn't have the sensibilities of a powerful mind. Think an early day *Austin Powers* - in fact it would not surprise me if this film influenced Mike Myers. John Candy plays the lead, Harry Crumb, kind hearted and completely oblivious character who occasionally has a lightbulb moment (or a bit of good luck) and actually comes good in the end.

It was written by Robert Conte and Peter Wortmann, directed by Paul Flaherty (Joe Flaherty's brother) and produced by Arnon Milchan and Frostback Productions - John's own production company.

Harry Crumb is employed to search for a kidnapped fashion model, Jennifer Downing (Renee Coleman), who is a daughter of a millionaire, PJ Downing (Barry Corbin). PJ Downing turns to a family friend, Eliot Draisen (Jeffrey Jones), for help. Draisen is the president of the Crumb & Crumb detective agency, he assigns Harry the job as he actually doesn't want the crime solved - for it was actually he who had Jennifer kidnapped. He is also in cahoots with Downing's wife, Helen (Annie Potts), who he is lusting after. Helen isn't interested in Eliot, but is certainly wanting to get her hands on the ransom money, she is however having an affair with Vince Barnes (Tim Thomerson) her tennis coach. Helen and Vince long to be together, so try to kill PJ several times and plan to intervene the ransom money and elope.

Crumb goes to Los Angeles to meet the Downings - and with his clumsiness doesn't make the best first impression. However Jennifer's sister, Nikki (Shawnee Smith), befriends Crumb and together they investigate. Detective Casey, played by John's dear friend Valri Bromfield, also arrives on the scene as his rival - only to dismiss and berate Crumb, as her investigative skills are far superior.

Eventually Eliot escapes to the airport, Buenos Aires-bound with the money, making the mistake of informing Helen of his plans. Both Helen and the tennis coach intercept him, take the money and leave him bound and gagged in a boiler room. Harry turns up in the nick of time to confront Helen, Eliot is found and confesses to everything, Jennifer is freed and the crime is solved. Harry then gets acclaim from everyone including Detective Casey and is then made president of Crumb & Crumb.

For John this film was a great opportunity to show the range of characters he could play and it looked like he had a lot of fun with it. With Harry being a private detective it was necessary for him to go undercover in various guises; a Hungarian Health & Safety officer for the beauty salon where the crime took place, an Indian Janitor to spy on Helen Downing via an air duct, a drag queen, and probably the funniest - a jockey! Imagine 6ft 3 John, dressed in a shiny jockey shirt, jodhpurs surrounded by professional jockeys (bearing in mind the average height of a jockey is between 4ft 10 and 5ft 6) getting stuck in a jockey sized telephone booth. For anyone that remembers John's character in *SCTV*, Angel Cortez - FBI Jockey, I'm pretty sure this scene in Harry Crumb was inspired from those sketches. Anyone being undercover and sticking out like a sore thumb without being spotted, is funny.

The film was put out via Tristar Pictures and later in interviews John would talk about his disappointment that Tristar didn't give as much marketing support as the film warranted. So much so when he asked if they could send over a radio advert for *Who's Harry Crumb?* to play on his radio show (*Radio Kandy*) - they sent a cheque for US$500 thinking they just had to pay for the advert to be played - it didn't occur to anyone in the marketing department that they actually needed to make an advert! He felt like the marketing execution on the movie was so poor that the movie suffered as a result.

Even though John was disappointed with Tristar, as per usual the cast and crew had a ball on set, and he included his friends wherever he could. James

Belushi turns up in a cameo role as a man on a bus, Joe Flaherty plays a doorman, and Tino Insana and Doug Steckler also feature.

Manny Perry who is a well-known stunt coordinator and stuntman in Hollywood, is occasionally pulled in to act, in *Who's Harry Crumb?* he played a cop in a car. He actually ended up working on four films with John; *The Great Outdoors*, *Uncle Buck*, *Who's Harry Crumb?* and *Home Alone*, and they became firm friends. In a recent interview conducted by *The Hannibal TV* with Tommy 'Tiny' Lister, aka in the wrestling world as Zeus/Deebo, Lister talks about John and Perry. Lister worked with John a few years prior to *Harry Crumb* in *Armed and Dangerous*. My timeline maybe a little off as I'm not sure which film is being referred to, but whilst we are talking about Perry I'd like to bring this story in. Lister could not sing enough praise for John Candy, he stated that the best human he had ever met was John Candy that "he was an angel". Lister told *Hannibal TV*, "If you had a problem, John Candy would find out and fix it for you, he'd pay for it, out of his own money and he won't even let you know he's doing it. I'll give you a good one. Manny Perry doubles me in all my movies... Manny's father died, this is what was told to me about John Candy. He sent the guy home in his private jet, put him in the best hotel in that City, kept paying him like he was the on set, had a limo sent twenty four hours, he paid for the funeral and told him to come back when he wants to. That's John Candy."

Lister continues to tell a story about a security guard that was behind on his rent and about to lose his apartment, John went up to the guy and gave him a hug, slipped US$10,000 into his coat pocket without him knowing. Even now John has passed over he is still looking after his friends, Valri Bromfield told me "When I get a residual from *Harry Crumb* I always say quietly 'thanks John, I miss you.' It is just like him to keep giving even after he has left us."

Speed Zone or *Cannonball III* as it was also known, was released in 1989, John and Eugene Levy had lead roles in this illegal cross country race comedy. Allegedly, John had known the movie wasn't going to be great, but the money was good and he knew by convincing his friend Levy to take one of the roles that they would have a fun time.

Buck Russell, Moley Russell's Wart

In 1989 one of John's most beloved and notorious characters came to the big screen courtesy of John Hughes. In the end Candy trusted Hughes so much he used to just ask Hughes "where and when?" if Hughes wanted him to play a part. Candy's instincts were never wrong where Hughes was concerned.

Uncle Buck is the story of a lovable rogue, devoid of responsibility and out for a good time, making a quick buck wherever he can. He's a nice guy but not someone you would want to give an important job to, unless it was organising a party. His long-suffering and increasingly impatient girlfriend Chanice Kobolowski (played by Amy Madigan) is constantly trying to convince him to settle down and get a regular job. One night Buck's Brother and Sister in Law, Bob and Cindy Russell (played by Garrett M Brown and Elaine Bromka) have to call on Buck when Cindy's father has a heart attack and they need to leave town to visit him. After frantically calling everyone else they know to look after their three kids, Maizy (Gaby Hoffman), Miles (Macaulay Culkin) and Tia (Jean Louisa Kelly) they have to reluctantly call Uncle Buck to help them out.

Buck drops everything in the night and drives over to the Russells' household whilst trying to remember the kid's names on the way (he thinks one may be called Jennifer - which delights his own daughter, Jennifer Candy, every time she hears him say it in the film). He actually does a great job of looking after the children albeit not necessarily a traditional one. He wins the hearts of his youngest niece and nephew quickly after lots of big meals – giant pancakes, ingenious ways of doing the washing (microwaving socks because he "can't get the god-damn washing machine to work") and being generally funny and respectful with them, they absolutely adore him. On the other hand Tia (Kelly) the eldest, a rebellious teenager gives him a run for his money, especially where her delinquent boyfriend, Bug (Jay Underwood) is concerned.

Bug is basically a scumbag and Tia can't see it, she thinks he's the coolest and she's in love, only to get hurt later at a party where he tries to pressurise her to have sex and ends up going with someone else.

Working with such a young cast came naturally to John, basically treated them like he would his own kids, "The whole attitude in acting with the two kids in the movie is based on my relationship with Jennifer and Christopher, and how I would deal with them. And I dealt with each one differently as I do with my kids, the one thing I never did was I never talked down to them at all". To corroborate, Jennifer, John's daughter has said in interviews that he was most like his character in *Uncle Buck*. The interrogation scene between young Culkin's character and Candy is genius – however the questions and answers passed back and forth was difficult for 8 year old Culkin to remember, Candy remedied this by telling Hughes to put the camera on his back. Candy would say Culkin's lines and Culkin would repeat it back, add in some cuts back and forth and the scene is perfect and hilarious. Culkin cannot remember that much about his time on Uncle Buck, but he remembers John Candy as being 'funny and fantastic', he also has a loose memory of John Hughes' birthday that year, Candy got a clown to come to the studio that day and Culkin believes there may have been a stripper at night but of course being a child he was not present.

During the early meetings Jay Underwood (Bug) remembers, "Us kids were kind of hanging out with Candy, when young Macaulay Culkin just blurts out, 'How much do you weigh?' Candy said something like 'Well who wants to know?' in a good natured way. Mac responded with 'My friends at school told me to ask you how much do you weigh?' At that point Candy just kind of good-naturedly got onto another subject! The thing about John is that he's humorous off screen but he's not always doing his 'schtick'. I most often refer to him as a super nice guy, big teddy bear of a fellow, kind and caring – a family man. He was just pleasant to be around. Totally unaffected."

Jean Louisa Kelly was only 16 when she got the part of Tia, "The first time I met John was at the screen test, I think. I had never had a screen test before, in fact, *Uncle Buck* was my first movie. John was friendly, relaxed and funny... I didn't know much about his work at the time. I must have seen some of his movies, but I was a theatre geek so films were not my specialty. John was always lovely, funny, relaxed and playful. From what I remember, it seemed easy to him... the whole experience was challenging for me because it was so new, such a different way of doing things, that I am sure he was doing his best to make me feel comfortable."

Although Bug literally was an annoying 'gnat' on screen, off screen Underwood is a lovely man and a huge Candy fan thrilled to be working on *Uncle Buck*. "I loved Candy's movies! My friends and I were always doing imitations of him. The first time I met him was at my second/last audition for the part. Originally Bug was written as a punk rocker so I had a friend do my make-up and hair, another that helped dress me in some of his punk clothes along with some jewellery I had from an after school special I did called *The Day My Kid Went Punk*. I knew I had to go to both my auditions completely in character or they'd never see me as the part. I had the spiked mohawk hair going on, leather jacket, all kinds of crazy necklaces and rings, motorcycle boots and I played the part as well. I remember John Candy asking me, 'So what's that thing there hanging around your neck? Is that some kind of animal or something?' I responded, 'It's the jaw of a rat, man' because it was – I had an actual jaw of some kind of animal, I'm not sure if it was really a rat, probably something a little bigger. To which he said something like, 'Oh, that's very interesting'. In any case, we read the scenes a few times and that was that. It was just Candy and Hughes at my audition, and maybe the casting director. It was awesome, I was so excited. I knew Hughes was supposed to be there, but I didn't know Candy was until I walked in the room! Both were kind and cordial."

Whilst filming Kelly turned 17, John bought her a massive cake with "She was just seventeen, you know what I mean" written on and gave her a Hard Rock Café jacket from Chicago. Kelly remembers, "Sitting in the freezing car in the suburbs of Chicago at 3:00 in the morning, doing our scene at the end of the movie where he comes to rescue me from the party. It's funny how you can have such intimacy with someone through acting – we never saw each other after the filming was done, but I feel close to John when I think of that night."

Underwood told me, "Working with he and Hughes was like living a dream to me – it was amazing! Hughes would always shoot the script but then do tons of improvisation. He would give you crazy things to try, wanted you try whatever you wanted and just let the film run out of the camera without cutting. It was great to play off Candy because he enjoys to work that way as well. The one scene I remember most was filming the trunk scene where he has locked Bug in the trunk of his car and then opens it up to reveal to Tia how he's duct-taped my hands and mouth. He proceeds to rip the tape off my mouth (which, by the way, on the first take really hurt as we were outdoors in a suburb of Chicago in the dead of winter) then I spit out a handkerchief at him and start screaming all kinds of mean and profane things at him. Hughes told me to say whatever I wanted to say because he could edit it the way he wanted later. So on one take I think I started calling him a fatso and things like that. After the take, Candy very politely said to me, 'Uh, we can lay off some of the fat comments okay?' To which I was like, 'Oh of course, sure, I'm sorry, no problem!'

It was obvious to Underwood that Candy and Hughes were very close friends, "He and Hughes were obviously great pals and I think their families may have been friends as well. Sometimes we would be setting up a scene with the lighting and camera, everything would be ready and we would be waiting on Hughes and Candy because they were in Candy's dressing room watching the hockey game on TV! On another occasion we stopped in the middle of shooting to all go outside (cast and crew) and watch one of Hughes' kids blast off a model rocket. It was a very relaxed set. Hughes and Candy, being who they were, could really call their own shots and I don't think the studio brass really gave them a hard time about anything. However, that's simply from my own outsider perspective.

"Shooting the trunk scene was my favorite as I got to do a lot of fun improv that Hughes kept in the movie. As I said it was cold and the first time he ripped the duck-tape off my mouth it seriously stung! My mouth was all raw and red. When we did the golf ball scene, they used a plastic golf ball that got thrown right off camera but when I fell onto the grass, the grass was frozen solid and so it started to tear up my arms, still it was so much fun!

"Filming was fun as well because we took over this giant, abandoned high school that had two gymnasiums which we used as sound stages; the classrooms were the dressing rooms, makeup, school, etc. and the crew road bicycles through the hallways with the school's main office area serving as the office for the production company."

John Hughes once said that "*Uncle Buck* was a perfect Candy script for me to direct, because he put himself into it".

There was one rare occasion when Candy and Hughes would come to loggerheads. One night during filming Candy went out and had a great time in the local pubs and bars in the area - this was mentioned on the local radio station the next morning, Hughes overheard and when Candy turned up for work (always on time) he was sent home, to Candy I'm sure he was just living his character - it's something Uncle Buck would have most definitely done in the most harmless way. Of course working and being friends, there was always going to be a fall out at some stage - this one was forgotten about quickly.

As per usual with Hughes films, they filmed a lot of scenes that sadly didn't make the final cut. Boom operator Greg Agalsoff remembers one, "A funny anecdote took place while we were doing *Uncle Buck*. John was talking to a few of us between scenes, and he said, 'Hey, watch this'. His friend, Frankie, was given a small part by Mr Hughes in which several of Uncle Buck's friends had come over for fun and frivolity and beer. Frankie was sitting on a sofa, feet up on the table and holding up a newspaper which he was reading. Candy said, 'Frankie, can you help me out? I think I left my script out in the motorhome. Can you go get it for me?' Without lowering his paper, Frankie bellowed, 'F**K you, you lazy ass! Get up and go get it yourself!' We were in tears. Candy, undeterred, and trying not to laugh, said, 'Aw c'mon, Frankie, my knee is bothering me and it's cold out there!' Frankie continued to hurl a litany of expletives that had us all writhing. John kept pleading, but to no avail."

I can't help but think this is why John loved Frankie so much, Frankie seemed to be with him for the largest part of his career, when Hollywood is so full of 'yes' men he knew Frankie was dependable, honest and wouldn't hesitate to tell him where to go if he felt like it. I think we all need a Frankie in our lives, for they make the most loyal of companions.

Polka, Polka, Polka

Apparently John Hughes had the idea for *Home Alone*, back when they were filming *Uncle Buck*. In *Uncle Buck* there is a scene where Buck's frustrated girlfriend Chanice (Amy Madigan), knocks on the door of the Russell's house. Chanice has been sent round by Buck to look after Miles and Maizy, whilst he's gone out to find Tia (who has strayed to a weekend party without permission). Miles is camped inside the house looking through the letterbox waiting for Chanice's arrival. The first time Chanice knocks, Miles looks and Chanice is out of sight so he closes the letterbox. Second time Chancie knocks, Miles looks and there are three scary looking men peeping back through the letterbox at him, third time, he looks again and it's Chanice.

So the three strange men (blink and you will miss them) depicts every anxious child's imagination. Allegedly for Hughes this sparked his imagination too. He wrote a script that would be *Home Alone*, about a child, Kevin McCallister (Macaulay Culkin), from a large family, accidently being left behind at Christmas time whilst the family go on vacation (due to a head count error). The whole film is then about Kevin coping on his own and also defeating some pesky house burglars determined to break into his home, whilst his family, mother in particular (played by Catherine O'Hara) desperately tries to get home to her son even though there are no flights.

Hughes asked John to do him a favour and have a cameo part in the film as Gus Polinski – the Polka King of the Northwest who was travelling with his band the Kenosha Kickers and is the sweet man that offers Kate McCallister a lift back to her son after hearing her plea in the airport. Hughes in fact offered John 1% of the royalties from *Home Alone*, however John advised he was doing it for Hughes, not for the money and kindly declined his offer. In hindsight he turned down a huge payday as *Home Alone* is the biggest grossing comedy of all time, cue the John Candy shrug of the shoulders and laugh.

John literally filmed his scenes in Home Alone in less than 24 hours whilst a driver was waiting in the car park ready to take him to his next job. The Kenosha Kickers (John's band) were actually *Eddie Korosa Jr and the Boys from Illinois*. They got the job as *Home Alone* was being filmed near to Chicago where Korosa's parents owned a very famous polka bar called Baby Doll Polka Club since 1954.

Korosa Jr. remembers spending a wonderful 18 hours filming with John, he told me;
"During scene set up I would take requests from John to play and sing polkas. While setting up we had most of the crew singing *Beer Barrel* polka, *In Heaven There is No Beer* polka, we even did the *Chicken Dance*.

"We got yelled at by Director, Chris Columbus, for having too much fun! He wanted us to stop playing. John Hughes was there and requested us to play one more polka. Fun!"

Korosa remembers that John was just so kind and talked to everyone, every single band member and told the funniest jokes.

There was a recent internet theory originating from Reddit that John's character, Gus, may actually have been the devil. For starters Kevin's mum is pleading for someone to help her get home and declares "If I have to sell my soul to the devil himself I will get home to my son" when John's character Gus pips in. Gus also plays the clarinet - the Devils choice of instrument is always woodwind according to the bible. The fact that they meet in the crossroads of Scranton Airport (to me this is tenuous, but lets keep going) means that Gus could be a Crossroads Demon. Apparently if you call the Devil at a crossroad he will come, I'm going to take people's word for that, I don't feel like I have to test the theory out!

I think both Johns (Candy and Hughes) would marvel at this thought and laugh it off without commenting either way. Maybe I shouldn't bring up that Hughes turns Del Griffiths into the Devil in *Planes, Trains and Automobiles*? As both Del and Neil are in a near death truck sandwich after Del is driving up the motorway on the wrong side, Neil looks at Del and

Del is cackling, cloaked in red, adorned with horns. Maybe there is something in this after all?

This wasn't John's only cameo that year, he also featured in *Masters of Menace* as a Beck's beer truck driver. In a much bigger part, one of John's most favourite projects to work on was also released, Disney's *The Rescuers Down Under*. Being a big kid at heart and loving to create characters, John was overjoyed to be the voice of Wilbur the Albatross. I suspect, just like *Radio Kandy*, he enjoyed the fact he could turn up for work, have some fun and not have to go into make-up.

Deliriously Happy

In August 1991 *Delirious* was released by MGM, a film about a soap opera writer, Jack Gable played by Candy, the soap "Beyond Our Dreams". Gable has an accident at the beginning of the movie and whilst being unconscious in hospital, wakes up in his own script where he can rewrite what happens at any time. It wasn't a box office smash but it didn't deserve the criticism it got from the critics, regardless of whether it was liked or not it was a complete love in for the team working on it.

It was filmed mainly in New York, directed by Tom Mankiewicz (*Dragnet*) with leading ladies Mariel Hemingway and Emma Sands and to John's delight a cameo from Raymond Burr. Raymond Burr was well known on stage and screen but most notably for playing the character *Perry Mason*, this was actually the last film that Burr ever worked on. The whole cast and crew got on wonderfully and from the moment they started on set to all the after work drinks they had a blast. John particularly got on with Tom and Mariel who became lifelong friends. Sadly Tom has passed away, but he did talk about his love for Candy in his autobiography, *My Life as a Mankiewicz*. "I used to bound out of bed to get on the set. Delirious was the single happiest experience I ever had. I loved everybody in it. I loved everybody on the crew. I loved everybody around it. John Candy was such a wonderful leader, and I felt I was a leader as well."

For John he wasn't only the lead, but he was the romantic interest too, being pursued and pursuing both Hemingway and Sands' characters respectively. This was a notable shift in Candy's career, he was showing new sides to his already diverse acting capacity.

Mariel hit it off straight away with John, they had a real spiritual connection and were just so comfortable with each other. "I think John had a lot of demons. I think when you are that kind of weight you have a lot of stuff going (on) and I think that he knew I had a compassion for covering up pain, because I came from such a crazy family, I think he felt that understanding." This was Mariel's first physical comedic role and she felt John aided her, teaching her in a way she taught herself, he would never tell her what to do he would just enable her. He also encouraged her: "He was a good audience, he laughed a lot".

Hemingway was worked on many different films and noticed something so different about working on *Delirious* with John. "He was just so generous; he couldn't have been more kind. I really loved him, I was not a person that liked to go to work and deal with people that had egos, problems issues etc." They had the same mentality, "We were like let's just get the job done, everyone here is making a difference, everyone here has a say in this without one cog we are askew and he knew that and I always felt like that. It's not about the big name actor, it's really about everybody else. He took care of people; he saw himself no different to anybody else."

Part way through the film John's character writes himself in as a great horse rider to woo both leading ladies, Hemingway had ridden all her life so she could do her own stunts, however John actually worried about riding horses so they got him on a mechanical horse to make it look like he was riding. For Hemingway it was one of her favourite memories "It was just hilarious and he was just so great at making fun of himself."

Delirious was no different to any other movie John worked on. He was always early to work and the last to leave set, he was always there, even if he wasn't needed, he just loved hanging out, like a little kid he was worried if he left he would miss something. "He was definitively one of the kindest humans I have worked with. He came early to work, he left after everyone had gone. He always took care of the crew and the cast, he loved working and he loved people. He was truly an amazing human being."

Musician and actor Mickey Stanhope was working as an extra on *Delirious* when he met John.

"I started out doing extra work in 1988, working on *Coneheads*, I got to know a lot of the comedians and did a lot of extra and stand in work. *Delirious* was just a couple of days of extra work, I got there and found out it was a John Candy movie, I had worked with Mariel Hemingway before on a TV show so I knew her going in but it was great to work with John."

The first day Stanhope was there, they were all standing around in tuxedos ready to film a party scene with Raymond Burr. "I started talking to Raymond who was very effeminate and he giggled like a girl, which made me laugh and John would crack up, he would fall over with laughter."

Stanhope was from Chicago and John had lived in the Old Town when he was training at Second City. "He said to me, 'You know where I lived? I lived on Curly Way.' He started telling me about his love for Curly from *The Three Stooges* and then he started doing impressions. We just reminisced about Chicago a lot and how much we loved Old Town. I told him about my band (*White Lighting, The Litter*) and he said I remember you guys. We just hit it off, the spark between us, we were similar sort of people, we could just talk for days."

Regardless of how the film did at the box office (it made just over US$5.5 million and cost around US$18 million to make), the cast and crew certainly won the prize with Delirious. Everyone was treated with the utmost respect, it was very low key and everyone got what they wanted. Mankiewicz was such an accommodating and a jovial director that his positivity just trickled down to everyone on set. At the end of every night's shoot they would all bundle in to a trailer, drink and listen to the stories Mankiewicz would tell them. John thoroughly enjoyed himself.

Forty

On 31st October 1990, John turned 40 years of age. He rang his agent Catherine McCartney and said "I made it", as he never thought he would, McCartney had lost her dad at a young age too, so they had discussed in length their worries. He always thought he wouldn't make it past his 30s, like his dad didn't, and yet here he was, a famous movie star, happily married with two beautiful children - living the dream.

John had lived his whole life like he was a ticking time bomb, saying 'Yes' to nearly every job in order to bankroll money for his family just in case something was to happen to him. He wanted to be sure he could look after them even if he wasn't around. Capital, savings, residuals from work - every dollar would help his beloved family. He went out a lot, lived a lot, loved a lot, just in case he didn't get to forty, so for John, this was a massive achievement and relief.

However with relief, after all those years of having that fear gnawing at the back of your head, anxiety can sneak in. Now I am not saying John never had anxiety before this stage, but certainly this is where it became a bit more overwhelming and he started having panic and anxiety attacks. In the 90s, mental health was still a taboo subject, however John, being as real and as human as he was, actually talked about his experiences of these attacks in several interviews. He also talked about seeing an analyst - which would be more commonly known as a therapist or counsellor - advocating them, saying he thinks everyone should have one and that he wished he'd seen one as a child.

John really wore his heart on his sleeve, warts and all. I think that's just one of the reasons why the general public and everyone he came into contact with just loved and related to him so much. It was ok, not to be ok.

As much as the anxiety crept in, I get the feeling that in other ways, with age and experience on his side, John was more confident. There is a wisdom that arrives when you turn forty, and certainly for John, new things were on the horizon.

Nothing But Trouble

Ahhhh. So, if you haven't watched this film, theoretically it should have been a box office smash. John, Chevy Chase, Demi Moore, Dan Aykroyd are the lead characters. Originally entitled 'Valkenvania', written by Peter Aykroyd (Dan's brother), Dan Aykroyd screen-adapted the script and directed the film. With this amount of talent it should have been a recipe for success, surely? Aykroyd's directing debut, *Nothing But Trouble* is a weird horror comedy, very much of its time and one of those films you either love or hate. You might get a feeling of which way I lean as you read on, actually hate is strong word, maybe bizarrely bemused would be a more accurate description.

A chance meeting in a hotel between bored financial publisher, Chris Thorne (Chase) and lawyer, Diane Lightson (Moore), leads to a road trip that goes wrong, when Thorne decides to take the scenic (or not so scenic) route, running a stop sign and speeding their way through the sleepy, creepy, town of Valkenvania. Chased and caught by the local cops, Dennis Valkenheiser (John Candy) and his cousin, Miss Purdah (Valri Bromfield), they are escorted to Dennis' 106 year old eccentric Grandfather, Judge Alvin Valkenheiser (Dan Aykroyd).

I get the feeling John did this film as a favour, he did that quite a lot, he would always help a friend out. He didn't just play Dennis in this film, he also played Dennis' mute sister, Eldona who was desperate to marry the lead character, Thorne.

Valri Bromfield remembers her time with John on set, "We had so many good times together. He was always fun to work with and he made me laugh so hard. When he was dressed in drag he hated it. I have a photo of us from Danny's movie *Nothing But Trouble*. John's in drag and I'm the dyke dressed like a cop - pretending to be his butch mate. John hated doing drag but he was so damn pretty. So, when I look at this photo I remember he had just been telling me he hated doing drag but in the photo he is smiling and doing the whole girl thing. He did it for the photo.

"When we shot that film we each had a cop car - his all tricked out on the exterior and mine, the deputy, just a plain cop car. But we shot in Valencia CA in the summer and it was about 120 in the shade. My car, by some miracle, had AC and his did not. He assumed, by the look of my car that I did not have AC either. So when I saw him sitting in his car, waiting to do the drive-through shot he was drenched in sweat. In my car the AC was blasting and my car temp was about 50. So I got out and walked up to his car and very seriously said "are you hot?" and he had a big reaction. I told him that I meditate to cool my body and that it worked. He touched my cool arm and was amazed. So I returned to my car and watched him. He was sitting in his car, his eyes shut, trying to cool himself, sweat streaming down his face. Then, he got out of the car, almost overcome with the heat. I motioned him over to my car, rolled down the window and he felt a blast of cold air. He did that thing where he would make a sound and lunge for you. It was so much fun to mess with him.

"John was great to work with. Generous. He never thought of himself as a star. But he was tough when somebody needed protecting. In *Nothing But Trouble* I had to shoot guns and rifles, and they kept sticking so the guy who was in charge of them started berating me for my inability to make them work. John gave the guy a kind of "make my day" speech. He just quietly stepped into the space between us, got in the guy's face, leaned down close, and spoke very softly to him. When he stepped away the guy looked like he had soiled himself and was extremely apologetic to me."

Typical John, looking after the people he loved.

In Tom Mankiewicz's book, *My Life as a Mankiewicz*, he talks about going to visit Dan and John on the set of *Nothing But Trouble*. Of course Mankiewicz had directed Aykroyd in *Dragnet* and John in *Delirious* and was good friends with them both. When he got there Aykroyd was exasperated.

"I walked on the set about two weeks in. Danny said to me, "I'm having some problems". Immediately, I saw what one of the problems was. All the actors had their own video screen. So they would look at their own takes and decide whether they wanted to do another one. Please! You can't do that. Danny said 'This is crazy. If I could quit, I would. Everybody wants to know everything. Two hundred questions a day: Is this okay? Do you like her hair that way?' "

I think the fact Aykroyd wasn't enjoying himself portrayed onto the screen. In fact watching it, I'm not sure anyone was really having a blast. However as I say, audiences either love or hate it. It was obviously a huge plot, with plenty of detail (maybe a bit too much detail), a massive budget, US$40 million in fact! With the prosthetic makeup for Aykroyd, making him appear elderly (and someone must thought it was funny to give him a nose the shape of a phallus), the "Mr Bonestripper" roller coaster ride - where the unwilling participants have been judged worthy enough to meet their demise for their crimes (less of a rollercoaster - more of an abattoir conveyor belt where all that is left at the end of the ride are the bones of those who rode). The crazy castle where the wrinkly, eccentric judge lives, to the scrap yard out the back where his two deformed adult baby grandchildren reside, Bobo and Little Devil (they kind of looked like Jabba the Hutt if he had legs). Bobo was actually played by Aykroyd too, they are in fact the reason why Chris and Diane actually manage to escape the hell hole - only to report them to the authorities and then realise the police were actually in cahoots with the judge. Confused? You will be. Oh did I mention 2Pac turns up part way through, with his band, *Digital Underground*, they had been pulled on a speeding charge, but they end up jamming with the judge?

But here is the thing. You win some and you lose some. I can see what they were trying to do, but I think everything just had too much detail and the detail lost the plot along the way. However, the film was certainly better for John being in it.

Hauled across the coals by critics, Aykroyd was awarded the Worst Supporting Actor Razzie at the 12th Raspberry Awards, John was nominated Worst Supporting Actress for his role as Eldona.

Good to know that things don't always turn out for the best of them, you just wipe the slate and carry on. That's the beauty of being creative, you just carry on with the next project.

Only the Lonely

Only The Lonely, written and directed by Chris Columbus saw John in another leading role with more of a romantic dramatic setting.

John plays Danny Muldoon, a thirty-something Chicago cop, still living with his mother, Rose Muldoon (Maureen O'Hara), who is loving but oppressive and does not want to let go of her adult son. When Danny finds love in a painfully shy, funeral parlour make-up artist, Theresa Luna (Ally Sheedy), Rose tries to do everything in her power to sabotage the relationship.

Until working on *Only the Lonely* O'Hara had retired from her acting career twenty years previously and was determined she would never go back. However Chris Columbus had written the role of Rose Muldoon especially for her. It took a while for Columbus to track her down and convince O'Hara she should read it, luckily for us she eventually did. She agreed to do the film if she met and liked Columbus as a director, and John who would be playing her son. It took her only a few minutes of meeting them in Chicago to decide, she loved them both straight away and she turned to John and said "All right, I will be your mother".

O'Hara remarked in her autobiography, *T'is Herself*, "The depth of John Candy's talent did surprise me. I didn't expect it to be so great. It didn't take long for me to see that his reservoir of emotion was deep, and that he was not only a comedic genius but an actor with extraordinary dramatic talent. I'm sure that even he didn't fully understand how good he really was. He reminded me a great deal of Charles Laughton."

The love and respect was mutual, John was thrilled to be working with such a huge Hollywood star, you can see in every interview they did together just how much John adored Maureen, and they remained good friends for the rest of John's life.

Jim Belushi who was co-starring in the film, always recalls the story of John's and O'Hara's trailer. Basically John had a huge trailer, O'Hara was given a honey wagon. A honey wagon is tiny, and certainly in John's eyes, an insult to O'Hara. John went to discuss this with the production team - he was told that they couldn't afford a large trailer for O'Hara as they wanted the money "on the screen". John couldn't believe this - O'Hara was in *The Quiet Man*!, John's reaction was to give O'Hara his trailer and he took the honey wagon - the production team were mortified and after a few days managed to find the money to accommodate both stars in the manor they should be accustomed to.

That was just so John.

Colleen Callaghan who is in her 80s (and still working in Hollywood as a hair stylist because she loves it that much) was brought in to do hair for *Only The Lonely*. "If anyone asks me who was my favourite actor or actress to work with in my whole career I always say John Candy. I never have a doubt about who is my favourite.

"I was told by this girl who recommended me to him (sic), she told me he was a hopeless case because he sweats so profusely that no matter what you do to his hair by the time he gets through the first five minutes he is going to be soaking wet. So I can't stand things I can't overcome. I did research before I even met him on every antiperspirant that I could find that had absolutely no residue hangover, no powder, no oils. The only one I found was something that they don't make anymore and I brought so much I still have some, it's the Clubman. When I first met him he said 'I know it is going to be pretty depressing for you, my hair is going to go wet immediately but do your best'. I soaked his head with Clubman, I sprayed it once and blew it dry, saturated his whole head again with the Clubman and blew it dry. Then I put my product on and blew it and did my thing.

"I was taught way back in the beginning of my film career by George Hamilton that a man's hair is as important as a woman's and he showed me everything he did to create that image that he had.

So I started on John's hair and gave it all the volume I could possibly do." Much to her surprise John slept through the whole thing. "When he woke up he looked in the mirror he said 'Oh my God, oh my God that's how I dream of my hair looking but it's going to go limp oh I wish there was a way it wouldn't' and I said, 'Well let's just see'. That night I went in, he came and said to me 'Listen, I hope you don't mind but I put you in my contract' and I said 'John I don't do that anymore' and he said 'what do you mean?' For the first 18 years of this business I was in eight contracts and I felt like an entourage. I'm from Broadway, I am a performer myself and I like to be a designer of the whole thing not just follow the instructions of one person, which is what you do when you are personnel, that person is the boss. I have had to go against what I know is right for the period because of what the actress wants because she owns me during that period. The first movie I did after I gave up being personnel was *Broadcast News* and I thought I had died and gone to heaven, I never worked so hard in all my life and that's what I loved and I have been doing it ever since. He said 'OK I understand, you can do everybody just do me too.' I said, 'Well if it is under those circumstances, OK' and that's how I worked with him after that."

John was so thrilled with his hair, Callaghan remembers, "It was so cute he said 'Colleen I woke up and I saw my dream come true and it's lasted me through the day, you can't take my dream away'. I have never forgotten that he was so sweet."

One thing that struck Callaghan about John was how he could be funny without being insulting or mean. "Comedians can use their comic ability to be very vicious, and that was absolutely taboo with John. He was the kindest person, comedian, I have ever known because it is so easy to use that gift to be edgy. He was very generous to other actors on the set. I can't even picture him saying something negative about somebody.

"I met John's family because he had a table at the Kennedy Center, we all flew to the Kennedy Center and his wife and the children were there. Very sweet, very quiet, the children obviously totally adored him. His wife, I felt, was so at one with him, it was very interesting, there was no show stuff, so many people put on a show but there was none of that. She was very grounded and definitely avoided the limelight, in fact I think going to the Kennedy Center was unusual for her. She stayed at home and took care of her children."

After the first week of filming of *Only the Lonely*, John showed up in an extended limousine with his staff to pick up Callaghan, he took her to her first ever hockey game in Chicago. Every single one of them was treated like celebrities, not just John. Once John trusted you, he would treat you like royalty.

Working on security for the film were two sisters who were full time police officers, Marie Ferrero and Patricia Ribaldo Ferrero (I'll refer to their first names so not to be confusing). In the 90s most police officers had to take a second job to make ends meet, often in private security. The firm that they worked for secured the security contract for Only the Lonely. They were filming in a very rough part of Chicago and the sisters would split 24 hours taking 12 hours each. They covered various locations including the front of the funeral home where Sheedy's character worked and lived, and the bakery where Sheedy's character spots the wedding cake she wanted.

Marie remembers, "The one building was supposed to be the bakery (where Ally Sheedy's character sees her wedding cake) and it was the most rat-infested building and the front was made to look like a bakery. When we worked the overnight shift it was the only access we had to a toilet and we would have to get out of the car and go into this building in the pitch black, it was horrible. It looked so beautiful in the movie, but behind that shop front it was a little scary, it was like condemned!

"But we both worked when they were filming, because we were protecting the equipment they had left there. They had various dollies, lifts and things like that.

"My personal experience with him (John), my most memorable time, was seeing him and how he would interact with the kids.

"A lot of times they filmed really really late, one, two, three in the morning. Filming scenes with Ally Sheedy, walking down the street or going into what was meant to be the funeral parlour and all that. So it was all different times of the day and night. We were introduced to him, he had two people there that were hired as private security that followed him everywhere. Usually when you are a security officer on any kind of movie set they don't really want you to approach the stars and we've worked a zillion movies, Mr Candy was just so friendly to us. He seemed like kind of a shy guy, which was kind of odd with his whole persona.

"The thing that stuck the most was one particular evening, it must have been two in the morning, he was practically in his trailer, this neighbourhood wasn't the best and there were kids, some with parents, some without, it didn't matter how late it was – you could tell he was really tired, when you watch these things being filmed you can see what a drudge it is, things being filmed over and over. He had a trailer down the block from where the hotel was and he was walking into the area to get there. He heard these kids calling his name, about five or six of them and he looked tired. Without even blinking an eye, and against his private security wishes, he turned around and talked to these kids for half an hour and signed every autograph. We are not talking about lovely little kids that live next door, we are talking about a very hardcore gang in the neighbourhood. He spent time with them, he signed every autograph, he never said no, I remember he signed shirts. Watching him, I was so impressed. I have seen major stars that wouldn't give you the time of day let alone stop to talk to children.

"He seemed like a person that would fit in anywhere and get on with anyone. Every time we saw them (John and Sheedy) together they were walking next to the bakery, they did the scene several times. In their down time they seemed to communicate and talk and laugh. She was much more reserved in my opinion, but she wasn't afraid at all, she didn't have personal bodyguards, she seemed like a real ballsy girl. They were both kind of reserved and quiet but they seemed to get on really well. It was a really nice movie set, after working on so many others you could usually feel the tension. It was a really relaxed movie set, completely the opposite from what I had seen before. He was a real, gentle, nice man. He was a real gentleman."

Of course working on opposite shifts the sisters could give me different stories. Patricia recalls, "We were filming on Morgan Street, his trailer was off to the side and I was doing security for the trailers. He had a big double wide, Maureen O'Hara had a big double wide and it was about 3am in the morning. Fans would keep their kids out there all night long. They were filming the scene where they all went out to dinner, where Ally meets Maureen O'Hara for the first time. Maureen O'Hara is a wonderful woman, she said it was nice to see women in jobs like mine, our guns were always showing. We filmed at 33rd and Morgan where the main buildings were. One morning they had lighting problems and they had them both in there for hours and hours and hours, whilst they were getting the lighting correct. He had been up for about twenty hours straight.

"One night I was out there, you could tell the man was exhausted, you could see it in his face. He had his bodyguards and he was stepping up into his trailer and he had one foot on the stairs, and literally a full Chicago city block away he heard this little boy (he couldn't have been more than 9 or 10 years), and all of a sudden you hear this voice from down the block shouting, 'Mummy, it's him, it's him!' You could see the look in John's face he was wiped out, he was like 'Ah man all I want to do is go to my trailer and go to bed'. He stepped up into the trailer, the kid came running up the street with this colouring book he wanted autographing. John Candy gave this huge sigh and he stepped down off the trailer and spent at least fifteen or twenty minutes with this little boy. Whilst talking to him he signed whatever he wanted him to sign, he talked to him about being a comedian and he was so gentle with this little boy who was completely and utterly star struck by what he was seeing. He couldn't believe he was meeting the real John Candy."

To me this conjures up images of a child meeting the real Santa Claus - just magical, the kind of memory that you would tell your grandchildren about.

"I was so impressed as he was exhausted and 99% of the actors I have worked with would have just gone into their trailer and ignored that little boy. I worked on *Backdraft*, *Next of Kin*, *Primal Fear*, they would not speak to us other than through their PA. But Mr Candy, every time he walked past you he would have a nice word to say to you, we were technically not allowed to ask for autographs but I do have an autograph somewhere from him. He was a real gentleman."

Patricia remembers watching O'Hara and John working together, "They seemed to have a very good relationship, they were always laughing and chit chatting. They would stand and talk and it was not the general movie set. It was a pleasure and a privilege to work that movie.

"The reason we were hired was because they had made these sets to look however they wanted them to look, and then by morning the gangbangers would have tagged everything off, spray painting. In that particular case it was the Latin Kings that would get out there, on Morgan Street anyway. On 33rd and

Morgan, the building they made into a funeral home was an Hispanic banquet hall and we used to break up fights in that banquet hall once a week. It was a problem because they would tag the set every night, then they had to sandblast the paint off, repaint it, then do their filming, which is why they had hired us.

"It was the most pleasant experience of my life, anytime any of them came past, even Ally Sheedy who was very quiet and reserved, John Candy, Maureen O'Hara, always had a 'Hello', it was one of the thrills in my life. For me I grew up on Second City so for me to meet John Candy, you got the impression if you walked up to this man and spoke to him he wouldn't complain about it, because he would walk up and speak to you."

There is a scene in the movie, when Candy and Belushi's characters lower a dead body out of a window down the side of a building with the fire hose. Part way down the fire hose runs out and the body drops to the ground. Patty remembers, "That is something that I have had to do in the City of Chicago, not from the height he did it. But the guy we had was 600 pounds and up several flights of stairs, without moving walls, it was the only way we could get him out of the apartment. I worked the streets for 20 years, I never took a desk job. The bottom line is, I have seen a really lot of horrible things in my time and then to leave my regular job and go and meet a man like John Candy who portrayed the Chicago police like a Chicago policeman. The humour they had to use around dead bodies, the humour is what gets you through it else you go home and cry. You see horrible, horrible things, there is nothing you can do about it so you either laugh about it or cry about it. He portrayed us with perfection! He could have been a Chicago policeman."

Well the lovely stories don't end there, Leo Crotty who was a Police Sergeant at that time, was also working on the film. I'll leave you with Crotty's story as it sums up this gentleman perfectly. "There were three features going on at the same time, there was *Curly Sue*, *Only The Lonely* and *Backdraft* all being filmed in Chicago. So I was working a lot, mostly on *Only The Lonely*. I'm a Sergeant so I was in charge of the police crew there, and one of the things that I do is make sure that the people in the movie are safe, so it's my business to know who is who. There was this one kid that kept going in and out of John's motorhome and he was there with, I assume, his parents. I asked one of the crew, I said, 'Who is this kid that keeps going in and out of the motorhome.' He said, 'Oh he's the star in the next John Candy movie and they want him and John Candy to get to know each other'. So I thought nothing more of it. Then later on that day I talked to the second assistant director, I said 'I understand that this kid is going to be in John Candy's next movie', and he looked at me quizzically and said, 'No not at all'. I said 'Oh who is he then?' He said, 'This kid has cancer and he wrote a letter to John Candy and told him he was a big fan of John's and that he had cancer, and asked for a signed photograph of him'. So John wrote back to him saying that he'd like him to come over here and see him make his next movie, which was *Only The Lonely*. John said 'I'll fly you and your parents here and pay for your expenses whilst you are here'."

This story has never been in the public domain before, it was never publicised because John was discreet and respectful, however I think it sums up his magnanimous spirit perfectly.

JFK

Later in 1991 John landed a role that would see him excel as a dramatic actor, he was cast in Oliver Stone's legal conspiracy thriller, *JFK*, a film about President John F Kennedy's assassination. John played Dean Andrews Jr, the eccentric attorney from New Orleans that Clay Shaw asked to represent the suspected assassin of Kennedy, Lee Harvey Oswald. He co-starred alongside Kevin Costner who played the lead, Jim Garrison, the District Attorney of Orleans Parish, Louisiana, who was investigating the assassination (as a side note, the real Jim Garrison actually played Earl Warren in the movie).

Go and find old footage and interviews of Dean Andrews Jr and then go and watch John Candy's performance, John did an uncanny and outstanding job. He perfected Andrews' dialect, persona and mannerisms to a T. In a recent interview with The Hollywood Reporter, John's Daughter, Jen, told them "He worked so hard on that. He had a dialect coach, and he worked night and day on that script. He was so worried about it, getting that accent down."

John wanted everything to be perfect for his role. Colleen Callaghan was working on Green Fried Tomatoes at the time, and recalled, "I won't give a movie up for something else someone has requested me on as I have committed to the production. He was starting JFK and he phoned me, 'Colleen I know you are working but can I send someone to pick you up in Georgia and take you to Washington to show the hair stylist exactly what you do with my hair?' I said, 'OK, if it's OK with the hair stylist', he said, 'I have already talked to her it's OK'. So I was picked up and flown there and I met Elle Elliot who was so gracious she said 'I have been dying to meet you, thank you so much', she ended up working with me on Benjamin Button where she was one of my co heads of department. It was a lifelong friendship that was created."

Director Oliver Stone was interviewed for a documentary about John called *To John With Love: A Tribute to John Candy*. Stone said, "I think there is no question that he could have had a significant, dramatic career. He could have gone on and done bigger and bigger parts, he was excellent as Dean Andrews."

Talking of dramatic roles, it was often rumoured that John had been approached to play Fatty Arbuckle in a biopic. Those rumours were in fact true, although he turned the part down. To me it was John's way of being respectful to Arbuckle, he was worried about misrepresenting him - with great power comes great responsibility and to portray such a character it would have to be done right.

Rob Salem had chatted to John about this part and had more of an insight for me, "I wanted him to do the *Fatty Arbuckle Story*. I think he was afraid of it. I think he was afraid of where it would take him. Out of all the Second City people he got the furthest the quickest, so he didn't really have the of comfort zone that they had - which was his precedence before them. So that whole fame trap, he was aware of that and very wary of that, and that is what killed Fatty Arbuckle. He told me he was afraid to go there."

To understand what John was afraid of I researched Arbuckle and I found his story heartbreaking. A naive and sweet man, made and ruined by Hollywood. The problem is people love scandal, whether it's true or not is irrelevant to most, and although it's seen as tomorrow's chip paper by some, it ruins lives and breaks hearts. So I get it John, but I am with Salem and I think you would have done Arbuckle justice with a phenomenal performance.

****

That year, John moved Frostback Productions to a large office in Brentwood, it even had its own bar - not just a corner bar but a proper public house style bar!

You Don't Get Glory If You Don't Have The Guts

Back in the early 70s John said to his agent, Catherine McCartney, that one day he "would own the Toronto Argonauts", McCartney thought he was joking. He wasn't.

In 1986 John met Bruce McNall. McNall was the new owner of the LA Kings hockey team, he had fingers in many pies and was hailed as a very successful businessman and entrepreneur. Bowled over by McNall's personality and status, John just loved hanging out with him and held him in great esteem. "John was a huge hockey fan and when I bought the LA Kings in 1986, he loved the team and he was a big star. One of my jobs was to make sure the celebrities were happy and came to the games and so we developed a friendship from there" McNall told me.

John had season tickets to the LA Kings and used to go regularly with his old friends Martyn Burke and Stephen Young. The three of them would go to the hockey games and have a lot of fun, but John would drive them absolutely crazy. There are three periods in a hockey game, each twenty minutes long and by the last ten minutes into the third period they would also get the feeling John would want to leave and they had an endless battle to keep him there. John however was the driver, he had a Mercedes and the other two had small sports cars so John was their ride, so when he wanted to leave they would have to go. Burke remembers, "We would get to about 18 minutes and John would say 'It's a one goal game', we would protest 'It could change', 'No, no nothing is going to happen'. We would head up to the parking lot and he would turn on the radio, all of a sudden the game had tied up and totally changed! Then you would have a Mercedes full of people going crazy - bitching and moaning. John would say this only ever happened one time, but it happened over and over again."

The great thing about the old hockey games was no one in the crowd cared who you were, so John would be sitting in the stands, Tom Hanks would be in his baseball cap further up in the arena and no one would bother them because everyone was just there for the game and it was just a good fun time. Burke noticed that changed when McNall came on board with the Kings and he remembers the day they met, "John was sitting in the stand, Bruce came up in the middle of a game with his entourage and he almost pulled John out of his seat, he wanted John to become part of his group. From that moment John started being seduced by things I wish he hadn't gotten in to. Bruce seemed like a nice, funny guy who seemed to be a guy who came up from nothing, hardworking, but it turned out he was a wonderful con artist. John wanted to become Bruce McNall, he wanted to be a sports magnate a sports empresario he started dressing a bit like Bruce, he started sitting in Bruce's private seats, he no longer wanted to sit in the stands with us."

John and McNall's friendship progressed over time, they would see each other at games and if McNall was holding any events he would invite John. John attended the Rookie of the Year 1987 awards in Los Angeles and according to McNall he was the life and soul of the party. McNall recalls, "He was very comfortable around all the players and they were starstruck and he was quite starstruck by them, he was very open to the players, he was very funny and made everything very comfortable." John was also made Celebrity Team Captain of the LA Kings which thrilled him no end. In 1988 John even did a series of funny ads for the Kings, "We had local television and John decides he is going to produce the ad. So he writes it up and gets a bunch of movie stars that would go to the games. He played himself and he would be in front of the camera and he would say, 'Hi this is John Candy, we are here at the LA Kings game, all big stars come to these games now.' And as he is saying this Tom Hanks would walk by, and John keeps looking around and says 'Well I can't see any right now'."

McNall disagrees that John idolised him, he thought it was more of the case that John always wanted to be more than he already was, "No matter how good John was, he always wanted to be better". He did admire McNall though, and wanted to dip his toe into the business world, something McNall could introduce him to. The pair talked about producing films together but nothing ever came from it. The first time they really got into bed with each other was to fulfil another of John's dreams.

In 1991 McNall was thinking about buying The Toronto Argonauts and asked John what he thought, McNall tells me "John was like 'Oh yeah I love it, it's phenomenal! I would love to be involved somehow'. He was all excited about it which of course gave me more enthusiasm, so I got excited about it as well. That's when I said to Wayne (Gretzky), 'Do you guys want a piece of this?' and that's what led us to buying the team. I don't think I would have done it without John's enthusiasm. It was impossible not to be infectious with him; if he got excited then everything was exciting."

McNall was very aware he wanted John to be protected; in fact they both had the same lawyer at that time, Skip Brittenham. "When we were looking at buying the Argonauts, Skip and I discussed it, I was like I don't know how much money this is going to take, so we decided to make sure John was capped at a million dollars so he could never lose more than that. So although it cost us much more than that, me and Gretzky ended up putting in millions and millions of dollars, John was always capped at a million dollars. In my mind we looked after him ok in that regards. Skip was very happy that he was taken care of." They actually bought the team for CAN$5 million, John and Gretzky took 10% each.

For John it was a dream come true, he didn't do much acting for the next couple of years, he had just finished filming *Only The Lonely* and took some time out to promote the Argos and the CFL.

Brian Cooper who had already worked with Gretzky, was introduced to McNall and John and appointed as Chief Officer of the organisation. For the next 12-18 months Cooper would find John working from his office for many days of the week. Cooper recalls, "As a Canadian and just a fan of comedy that is how I knew John. A client of mine at the time, Wayne Gretzky, partnered with John in co-owning the Toronto Argonauts, a team that had been around over a hundred years, they had a strong following. John grew up loving the team. They bought it and then asked me to come on board, I came on as Chief Officer of the organisation and John was partnered with Bruce McNall and Wayne Gretzky as the three owners.

"So John at that time had finished a movie with Maureen O'Hara and he had a large gap of time between that movie and anything else. So he sort of spent a good two to three year period of not making movies and he became completely enthralled and happy to become a fan of the Argos and help out in any way that he could. So for a good 12-18 month period John would come into the office, not every day but four days a week. So it became, a comedian sits down in my office and helps run a football team. Now when I say helps run, he was certainly providing a lot of leadership to the rest of the staff and certainly comedic release. He was truly, truly passionate about this club.

"So he would come into the office and we had a working relationship that then became a friendship. Over the time I learned something people don't realise – just how intelligent John was. Whether it was history, religion, politics, comedy, film or sport he knew not just a little about a lot, he knew a lot about a lot. I don't know if it was from reading or what, but he was so intelligent and I loved that side of him.

"His passion that he wore on his sleeve was phenomenal. He used to barnstorm across this country to every away game and there was a blackout at the time. If you hadn't sold enough seats to sell out the stands then they would black out the television production of the game in the market to encourage people to go to the game. Well he would go out two days before the game and would get on every news show, every talk show and tell people to come on up to the game, 'We are lifting the blackout'. And he did it everywhere he went. He would walk up and down the sidelines – and this would be the opposing teams fans they would just stand and clap for this great iconic Canadian.

"When Wayne called me up initially he said he wanted me to come and meet John. So we had a meeting, we started talking about possibilities, what I thought of the team, what I thought I could do with the team and within a two week period I had left my own company and had starting working with these guys and then I saw John almost every day."

John got to know all the players, when he first met them he gave them his number and said to them that if there was anything they needed, just to call him. The Argos and the CFL in particular had been struggling, there were TV blackouts. John would get up at 4am two days before a game and relentlessly promote. He did interview after interview, never wasting an opportunity to sell tickets, John worked as hard as the players, if not harder and he did it all with his own money. His work quickly paid off.

The first Argo game of the season Cooper said to John "We're going to do an opening night", of course as soon as he heard those words John wanted to put on a show. John got Dan Aykroyd and Jim Belushi to come down and do the Blues Brothers, he flew in friends including Martin Short and Mariel Hemingway, he also totally broke the CAN$20,000 budget they had and the eventual bill was over $90,000. "There wasn't a budget he didn't like to break, that became a little difficult for me, I didn't want to dampen his enthusiasm and passion, plus it was a great idea! Jimmy Belushi, Danny, the opening night was a phenomenal night, the write ups said that we brought entertainment and sport together and we made a big bang in the city."

When I interviewed Mariel Hemingway, she remembered this night as "one of the best nights of my life".

That night Cooper stayed up with John and Aykroyd till four in the morning, Aykroyd owned a bar with a rooftop private area. Cooper sat under the stars watching John and Aykroyd just riff and riff backwards and forwards thinking to himself "life is just wonderful".

The players took to John immediately, he loved every single one of them. Cooper told me, "He was the most beloved owner ever, he would have given them the shirt off his back. He would listen to them, he would pray with them, as some of the guys were religious, he would help their families. I remember one of the things he did as he wanted to build the pride in the team, he went out and had forty leather jackets made and personalised with the players names and games on, the jackets at the time must have been around CAN$300 each. He was generous with his time and generous with his money. He was truly interested, it wasn't bullshit, he was truly interested.

"Then he would just talk football with them and just talk to them. He would be on the sidelines watching the games. If a player got injured, he would be the first in the locker room saying 'don't worry your career is not over, we are going to get the best doctors for you'. He was that way with the entire staff."

Wherever they went the opposing fans would boo the Argos as hard as they would boo anyone, but when John Candy walked out on the side-lines the whole stadium would erupt. John was like a Roman Emperor. Everyone would jump to their feet and just cheer, even just a lift of his eyebrow would set them off. He spent hours signing autographs, talking to people, being seen, he turned every single game into an event and the buzz was palpable.

Just like for the Kings, John would often do these 30-second commercials for the Argos, selling tickets with his wonderful comedic talent. In one advert John had made stick figures of various celebrities he knew and was acting as if he was talking to them. It was their face cut out on a stick. "Hey, Tom Cruise are you coming to the game?" and he would do different voices for everyone.

Cooper recalled, "People would be screaming out Uncle Buck and his other characters at the game. He was great when you asked him to go in to character on any show, he would go straight into character. We took him to a restaurant at the end of the night, we would have a dinner and he would be back there with the cooks."

John stayed up a lot, he would happily stay up till four in the morning and if they went out for dinner after a game he wouldn't just end up in the kitchen he would also be waiting tables. On top of helping the staff and the inevitable promotion of the establishment, he would also leave them a very generous tip.

As well as Candy being on board a very important and expensive signing was made to the team, Raghib "Rocket" Ismail. McNall outbid the NFL to bring Ismail to the CFL - he was given a contract that could earn him up to US$26 million over a four year period (at the very least he would walk away with $18.2 million). This was unheard of, all CFL teams were capped at earning CAN$3.8 million per year, Ismail was earning US$4.55 million per season - on the exemption that he was a 'marquee player'. This made Ismail's salary the highest in Canadian and American Football history at that time. Fortunately, he was worth it.

With the talent on the field and John's enthusiasm on the sidelines there was real hope for the team.

One of Cooper's favourite memories of Candy was in Edmonton, "We had won the game and I said 'John that was unbelievable' and he looked at me and said 'It's not about the moment, it is about the journey we are on and it is going to unbelievable'. He knew we were going all the way, it's not just about what had just happened. I just looked at him and he gave me a big smile and grabbed me in a headlock and said 'Let's go'." So you may wonder what it's like being in a headlock by John Candy? Cooper knows,

"Well I was six two, he was tall but also big, but he was like a friendly bear."

John and McNall would socialise a lot, "We would go to dinner together, we had a beach house and John and his family would come over and play there, we would sometimes watch the Argos games there. Hockey games we would go to around 40 events a year. Rose was just a very unassuming lady, not a typical Hollywood wife, just a normal lady, the kids were great fun kids. Just a normal family, you would have thought they were just a working class family, not stars in anyway shape or form."

John talked to McNall about the movie industry, he was frustrated by the process. John was so creative and had so many projects that he wanted to do but he couldn't get them off the ground. He felt like Hollywood had pigeonholed him and that he thought he had a lot more to give. "Both *Only The Lonely* and *JFK* were more serious roles and that's what he really wanted to do, and I think he would have done had he survived."

John had reignited the CFL. The Toronto Argonauts were working as a team, the energy and good feeling flowed. That year they went on to be undefeated at home and even won the glorious 79th Grey Cup Championship against the Calgary Stampeders. It was like a fairytale - everything they touched turned to gold and everybody was having a ball.

Cooper remembers, "First of all it was fantastic that we won it, we were undefeated at home. John used to walk up and down the sidelines and pick up one of the players helmets and hold it up in the air with the big Argonauts 'A' on it and the whole crowd would stand up. But when we won that at the end he made it all about the players. Whilst he loved winning and he loved the team he made it all about the players and never took any of that glory for himself. John threw a huge party for everyone and paid for it himself.

"We were in a hotel, we had all the players and families there and John had asked me to speak as the President, I said 'John needs to get up here'. John got up and started to get emotional. He may not be a player, he wasn't the only owner and he did not run the team, but he was the heart of the team and every player there would say the exact same thing."

However much he was enjoying himself, at some point John needed to go back to work.

John featured in *Boris and Natasha: The Movie* (a film about Rocky and Bullwinkle's nemeses) starring his old pals Dave Thomas and Andrea Martin.

He also took one of the leads in *Once Upon a Crime* a thriller, mystery, comedy directed by another friend and Second City alumni, Eugene Levy. John was in great company starring alongside Jim Belushi, Sean Young, Richard Lewis, Cybill Shepherd and Ornella

Muti. Set in Monte Carlo, John played Augie Morosco, a gambling addict, who, like everyone else in the film, becomes a suspect in the murder of a millionaire. Unfortunately *Once Upon a Crime* got a mixed reception and was panned by the critics. For me there was just too much going on within the story and it got lost within itself, there are some funny moments though and like with all the films that weren't highly acclaimed, John's performance always made them better.

Being the 'Whooooooole enchilada', John would also play an uncredited cameo as an enthusiastic sports commentator in the sports comedy, *Rookie of the Year*, directed by Daniel Stern.

But something bigger was on the way...

A Gold Medal is a Wonderful Thing

Cool Runnings was loosely-based on the story of the original Jamaican bobsleigh team who competed in the 1988 Winter Olympics in Calgary, 'loosely' being the operative word. The real Jamaican bobsleigh team were such an inspiration, just as they are in the film, they even use some of the original crash footage for the ending, but that is where most of the similarities end. Not that it matters, both are inspirational in different ways.

The rights were originally sold to Tristar Pictures, who later merged with Columbia and that's where producer Dawn Steel got involved. Originally the working script was called *Blue Maaga* (which means "serious trouble" in Jamaican) and was pitched as more of a sports drama than a comedy. Leon Robinson who played Derice Bannock and Doug E Doug who played Sanka Coffie were originally shown the script three years before filming started, two different Directors had been employed before Steel left Columbia and convinced Walt Disney Pictures to commission the picture. Jon Turteltaub was the eventual director.

The film's version of events start with Derice racing to qualify for the 100 metres, 1988 Summer Olympics. Derice falls along with fellow runner Yul when Junior (also competing) trips and falls, taking them both out. Desperate to go to the Olympics Derice hears about an old friend of his dad's, Irv

Blitzer. Irv was trying to recruit runners for his bobsleigh team years ago, he had won two gold medals, later on in his career he was disqualified for cheating at the 1972 Winter Olympics and had retreated to Jamaica to become a bookie. Derice finds Irv and after a struggle convinces him to coach the first ever Jamaican Bobsleigh team. The other three members of the team are made up by Jul, Junior and Derice's best friend, 'the best pushcart driver in the whole of Jamaica', Sanka.

"We were looking for someone to play an ex-Olympic Gold Medallist and a tough grumpy coach and the last person I would have thought of was John Candy." Turtletaub told me.

Turtletaub had not actually thought of John because his physical appearance was not typical of an Olympic athlete, in Turtletaub's head the part was more suited to someone like Kurt Russell (who actually ended up playing an Olympic coach some years later in a sports docudrama, *Miracle*). However, this was Turtletaub's first time directing a movie for a studio and it was actually Jeffrey Katzenberg, the Head of Disney Studios that suggested John Candy. "Jeffrey said 'what do you think of John Candy?' I said 'Sure!', it was Jeffrey Katzenberg –I thought it was a good idea to agree. Recreating some accurate portrayal of the Olympics, I thought this is crazy, but I really underestimated John's emotional power and dramatic ability to make it work."

Turtletaub was not the only one to have doubts about John playing the role. Leon Robinson who played the lead, Derice Bannock, was also unsure when he heard the news. "I didn't think John Candy was right for this role, they were also talking to Scott Glenn. I thought he would be much better, much more serious guy and then they told me it was going to be John Candy and I was like what? But whilst making the movie and after seeing the movie I could never imagine anyone else playing that role but John."

Rawle D Lewis who ended up playing Junior Bevil, the posh boy from a rich family trying to prove himself, was actually a reader on the script whilst they were auditioning. No one could play the part of Junior as well as Lewis so eventually he was offered the job. Hanging out as one of the readers, Lewis was privy to production banter and heard that John Candy was actually calling the studio and production team pushing for the part of coach Irv Blitzer, he even took a US$300,000 pay cut because he wanted the role that much. Being a massive John Candy fan, Lewis was thrilled John was on board.

Lewis recalls "So when we met John he said 'They don't understand what they have got with this movie, I am from Canada and I saw what happened, this movie is very spiritual, very powerful, they have no idea what they have here'. He had a meeting with all of us (the guys who were playing the bobsledders) he gave us everything we wanted, he made us something to drink, he made us very relaxed and then as he drank more he started to be really honest. He was saying they don't really know what they have here; this is such an uplifting movie. 'They are laughing at me for taking a pay cut, but I am from Canada and I was there.' "

John gave the young actors a pep talk, he told them that they could all go off and do their own thing if they wanted to, however he thought it was a good idea for them all to become friends, that if they got know each other it would show on camera and make it more believable. He also gave them gifts that he thought would be useful for their character preparation, he gave Malik Yoba, who was playing Yul Brenner, a CD full of music, Lewis was given pictures of the original bobsleigh team and a copy of Jimmy Cliff 'The Harder They Come'. Yoba remembered "He was the sweetest guy. He taught us to make every scene count - we are only as strong as our weakest link. If they don't believe me, they won't believe you. He chose music for each one of us, and invited us to have dinner at his suite. He gave us all CDs he had made for our characters."

John asked the young toboggan actors about themselves, they drank, laughed and chatted; he wanted to know everything about them. Part way through the meeting they told John how old they were, he exclaimed "I gotta tell you, screw you guys, I'm 42!". John forewarned the young actors that they had around half an hour before the production team would come in, they didn't want them all to get too close without their supervision in case they banded together. They all looked at John as if "It can't be that bad" and John gave them the look of "Trust me kids, I have been in Hollywood long enough". Lo and behold, 30 minutes later there was a knock at the door from the production team.

The day before filming John rang his old friend and costume designer from his *SCTV* days, Juul Haalmayer, "John called me and I was about to start a comedy pilot here in Toronto and he said 'Juul I need you in Calgary', I said 'John, what are you doing? I am about to start a pilot in Toronto' and he said 'I am doing a movie for Disney called *Cool Runnings*', I said 'What's involved?', he said 'Five weeks in Calgary, five weeks in Jamaica', 'When does it start?' He said 'It starts shooting tomorrow', I said 'John I can't pull a movie together in a day', and he said 'No I just need you to be here, so give Disney a call tell them what your rate is and get out of the pilot'. So I cancelled my gig on the pilot and I ended up being his dresser on *Cool Runnings*. He felt comfortable with me. That was really fun."

On set, Turtletaub along with many of the actors were fairly green, for a lot of them this was their first big feature film. John was like the father figure although he came over as more of a 'fun uncle', he made it easy for everyone and taught them a lot about professionalism and etiquette on set. He would walk into a room and everyone would just light up "Because the room was more fun with John in it", here you have this totally unaffected bona-fide movie star that is wonderful and respectful with everyone. Haalmayer commented to me that from the early days of *SCTV* to years later working on *Cool Runnings*, "John never, ever changed, never". John hung out on set a lot, the walk back to his trailer was a real schlep, he could have gone back and forth making everyone wait for him, but he never did. He loved being involved and as long as he had somewhere comfy to sit he was happy to spend all day on set, which was a boon for Turtletaub as he felt he always had a really funny buddy on site and John was always available.

The director also observed that he thought John had the 'niceness disease' where he just couldn't say no and would always make others happy even if it was at the detriment to himself, he would "put his own needs second, especially when dealing with the public". Turtletaub went to a Calgary Flames hockey game with John, "He couldn't walk two steps without being surrounded. All he wanted to do was go to the bathroom or go home and it was this non-stop barrage of people and it would cause him a huge amount of anxiety, but he stopped and he was pleasant and kind to every single person. I think he swallowed all that frustration and put all that inside, rather than lash out, or be in a bad mood, or yell at people, or finally snap, he kept it all inside. I think that stuff percolated inside him and he would have huge conflict with the fact that he would be in a bad

259

mood, or that he would be upset and he never felt it was OK to be angry. But as a result he was kind of torturing himself by beating himself up about it. He did take care of everybody, he was cursed with this, his lack of happiness was a curse, the reason he smoked and the reason he drank was his inability to be shitty in front of other people. But then he would beat himself up for having those feelings by drinking, smoking and eating."

There was one time on set when John was angry though, and of course it was to defend others, not himself. Lewis told me that he and Doug where running five minutes late to set one day and the assistant director screamed at them, like really screamed at them, John was just behind the young actors but slightly out of sight and heard everything, he got right up in the AD's face and said "DON'T you EVER talk to ANYONE like that again", the AD looked like he had soiled himself, apologised and everything was nice from there on in.

Of course there was still time to joke, Turtletaub said "He would tease me, I would give him direction and he would say 'you are not the boss of me', then he would go ahead and do whatever I had suggested or at least try it. The only time I ever really got him to admit I was his boss, we were in Jamaica and my parents had flown in a hard kosher salami from the United States and we had smuggled it into Jamaica, plying him with it I got him to admit I was the boss of him."

According to the production team John was really fun but he wasn't one of those guys that was 'on' all the time, he wasn't always performing for people off set and to Turtletaub the most impressive thing was the way John would laugh at other peoples jokes, "You don't see that in comic geniuses, they either don't react at all, or they smile and say 'that is funny'. But he would delight and laugh and enjoy and make other people feel funny and that is such a gift to give to people as his opinion matters so much."

At times the shoot could be quite physically challenging, during the scene when the toboggan team were learning how to toboggan down a grass hill in a pushcart, there was plenty of up and down that hill during filming. It was physically hard on John, running down wasn't so much of a problem although he had bad knees, walking back up was hard, but then it was hard for everyone and the whole team made a point of getting those scenes out of the way very quickly. As previously stated, John was large however generally he was very physically fit for someone of his size. Robinson commented to me "He didn't seem to have any health problems as such, yes he had a very strong appetite and I think if anything he seemed to be gaining some weight. But other than that he seemed to be relatively healthy. His fitness for his weight seemed pretty good at that time." According to Turtletaub John was well aware of any physical limitations he had and he went out of his way that it never became an issue when filming.

There are two points where *Cool Runnings* makes me cry. The first is a scene between Robinson and John, when Robinson's character Derice, asks John's character, Irv, why he cheated in 1977. Robinson told me the scene didn't take that long to do, they were both well-prepared and the chemistry was very good between them both which made for a very sincere and real performance.

The second is at the end of the film when the team crash, after the toboggan finally comes to a standstill and it's apparent everyone in it is ok, the team get up and carry their toboggan to the end whilst the crowd slowly clap into a great applause. Coach Irv runs down to check his team and he hugs Derice and they thank each other. That hug was not scripted and according to Robinson it was "very warm to be hugged by John Candy, he was a really good hugger. That was just a moment, that wasn't a scripted moment it just happened on camera, we just hugged – it captured and it was real."

I'm getting teary-eyed right now just thinking about that scene, it's such a powerful moment of love and hope and makes me cry like a baby when I watch it. Maybe add in the fact that this is the last John Candy film that would be released in his lifetime, he should be mighty proud of it.

 "A gold medal is a wonderful thing. But if you aren't enough without it, you'll never be enough with it" - Irv Blizter, Cool Runnings.

John, you were so believable in this role, I really hope you knew you were most certainly enough 'without it'.

Back to that tangent...

So remember Ken Tipton, the guy who owned the video stores and was John's stand-in on *Planes, Trains and Automobiles*? Well here is a little more to that story. So it is 1993, Tipton's life has been turned upside down, his business has gone bankrupt, his wife is divorcing him, he had been arrested and although was found innocent, he cannot get a job anywhere. "I thought f**k it, I had acting experience, so I moved to Hollywood. The way Hollywood works is no one makes it overnight, you need the SAG (Screen Actors Guild) Card - and in order to get it you need to do background extra work on the non-union side of acting. On these jobs you don't get lines, you might get actions, if you work as an extra you might get a line, then you are eligible for your SAG card or you can get three vouchers and then you can apply.

Tipton was really struggling to get any work when he remembered what John Candy had said to him, that if he ever got serious about his acting to give him a call. Unfortunately that turned out even harder than it sounded. Tipton would call John's agent, send faxes, leave messages, contact John's attorney and no one would ever respond to Tipton, he just couldn't get past the gatekeepers. Tipton kept wracking his brains on who to contact and who could help him. Eventually he thought of Dawn Steel, the producer of *Cool Runnings*. Tipton recalls, "I sent a fax to Dawn Steel and I got a letter back. Dawn says she totally understands and she can help me contact John Candy, she said to meet her at a book signing (her new book at the time was *They Can Kill You but They Can't Eat You.*)" Tipton gets in line, pays his $20 for the book, then introduces himself to Steel advising he was the guy that had asked for help and that he would like to meet later. Steel said, "well everything you need to know is in the book." Tipton tells me, "So for US$20 this lady snookered me for buying her book. So I finally read the book. It told me how she got started, the book is a brilliant, beautiful book on how Hollywood works, it's a big bubble - it's all about relationships.

"In one part of her book Dawn talks about needing a mentor to get into Hollywood, someone that will help you. So I thought I will just ask John to be my mentor, mentors don't do anything apart from giving you advice, no bullshit - but you need to contact that person and you need to find any way you can, you just find a way.

"John was genuine in his (original) offer (of help). So there was a service back then called Baseline, which was an online database that had everyone's contact details on it. If you wanted information Baseline had it, but it was expensive, I spent US$1700 in one month doing research on John Candy. Sifting through it, it went through all work etc, then it says he's part owner of Toronto Argonauts football team. So I look into that, one partner is Wayne Gretzky - Wayne is married to Janet Jones - Janet is from St Louis and her mother was a customer back in the video shop days. So I found Janet's mum, she remembered who I was and she gave a letter to Janet to Wayne to John. I heard nothing for 6 weeks. One day I get a call on my beeper, I pick it up, it's John Candy, 'Hey Ken, it's John Candy, What you doing in Hollywood? You need some advice, give me a call'. I got my questions together, I rang John and it went to voicemail, he called me back a few days later."

Ken told him what had happened and John gives advice on how to get a SAG card.

"John said, 'This is what you do, you go down to the LA film office and you find out what permits are filming on the weekend, you need to find a shoot that is as far away from the city as possible on the weekend. You will find out where it's shooting, you are going to show up and introduce yourself, just say 'I am not on your call sheet but I'll just sit over here until you need somebody and if you need somebody I will be ready to work'." When Ken asked why, John said, "Well they have a lot of SAG extras, that have got their SAG card, sometimes they don't show up especially if it's the weekend and far from the city - and that was it."

Ken did just that, he showed up at all the sets he could. "I found this one that they were shooting over the weekend, 20 miles outside town in a quarry, it was *The Flintstones*."

Ken shows up, does what John said, and advised the assistant director (AD) that John Candy is his mentor. Ken sat in parking lot, night after night, fourth or fifth night. "I bought a bucket and water and starting washing all the windows of all the cars, the AD saw I was being cool and thanked me for cleaning crap off their windows. One night he says to me
'Tipton, put your bucket down, go to wardrobe and get some buffalo gear', and I was in".

OK, hang on right there, we will be back with the final episode in the trilogy later.

"Surrender Pronto, or We'll Level Toronto!"

1993 was also the year John popped his directing cherry! His PA and Chongo, Bob Crane, had written a screenplay with his partner Kari Hildebrand, *Hostage For a Day*. They had sold the screenplay to Fox as a TV movie. John had agreed to direct it and have a cameo part as Yuri Petrovich, a Russian terrorist. Filmed in Toronto, John loved taking control back on his old stomping ground. He recruited Second City alumni George Wendt (*Cheers*) to playing the main protagonist, Warren Kooey, a man broken by his wife and his job, who is desperate to escape his mundane life. Kooey fabricates being held hostage by a Russian terrorist to extort money for a new life, and calls the SWAT team in (who turn out to be incompetent). In a strange turn of events, Kooey is then actually taken hostage by two Russian terrorists, one of whom is Candy.

Bruce Appleby was brought in as the key hairdresser for *Hostage For a Day*, he told me about his time working on set with Candy. "The whole crew loved him, it didn't matter what they were working on, he treated everyone the same. He was so generous with everyone - even the fans that came to see him, in the end they had to employ someone to stop the fans from interrupting the shoot. He was always bringing us surprise presents, Argos football jackets and hats, pen sets, gag presents, he would give us something every week. He was one in a million. I had never worked with anyone like him, before or after.

"He seemed to love directing and he told me he would love to come back to Canada and make more films here, to leave LA and the USA. He was such a proud Canadian".

Over twenty years after that initial Colgate advert, Jim Henshaw went to see John on the set of *Hostage*. John was soon to be starring in a film that would be using the same studio as *Top Cops*, a TV series Henshaw was working on. He went to meet John and producer of the new film, *Canadian Bacon*, to negotiate studio time. Henshaw was unsure if John would remember him, "I walked down to the set and John pointed at me, hollered my name and came over and gave me a hug. Then he said 'are you hungry?' and I said 'sure' and he walked me into the craft service truck and made one of the largest sandwiches I have ever tried to eat in my life! He was just talking a mile a minute. He made three sandwiches, one for me, one for his line producer and one for himself, and there was just layers and layers, it was his own secret recipe and concoction and he was really proud of it.

"In that 20 years he hadn't changed a bit. It was just really nice. That time, he really reminded me of why I had gone into the business in the first place. He had this ability to have fun, that feeling of 'we are here to do something special even though we don't know what it is'. And we started walking around set and he started describing to me what *Canadian Bacon* was going to be."

Hostage For a Day would be released April 1994.

Shortly after they wrapped *Hostage For a Day*, production started on *Canadian Bacon*, it was the first time documentary maker, Michael Moore, dipped his toe in the water of satirical comedy. John starred as the main character, Sheriff Bud Boomer (Sheriff of Niagara County), alongside Rhea Perlman, Alan Alda, Kevin Pollak, Bill Dunn and Rip Torn. Alda plays the President of the United States, he's low in the opinion polls and wants to orchestrate an event to win back some popularity, as well as increasing war and crime to generate income. Looking at those previously defeated, they decide to start a war with Canada after a fight breaks out at a hockey game - they see their opportunity to build propaganda, escalate it and give the people something to fight for.

This was another Marmite film, some love it, some can't stand it, a few are in the middle with their opinions, some may say it's like Moore had a crystal ball - but we aren't getting political here, it's not what this book is aboot!

Kevin Pollak talked to me about the time he spent with John. He had been a long time fan of John's he had heard lots of great things about him, did he meet up to Pollak's expectations? "And beyond! He was super generous, very gregarious and funny, open to improvise, just a very generous actor. You sensed immediately John was there to have fun and everyone would have fun around him."

Pollak had a very sweet memory of John that he shared with me "One of the most interesting conversations we had - he was having a cigarette one day on set and he said how his father had died from a young age from genetic heart failure / disease. He said, "I've known for a long time that I'm not long for this life because of this genetic defect. I just kind of decided to live to the fullest. So I have done a lot of projects I may not have done, just so I could bankroll some money for my family, and I didn't really expect to live this long." Pollak felt that John was explaining in the most polite and Canadian way that he knows he shouldn't be smoking or drinking etc. but he wanted to justify his reasons.

****

Sadly all was not well with the Argos, they were in financial trouble. Brian Cooper told me, "You know what, the team was losing money. Bruce McNall went to jail afterwards for fraud. I was running this team and I had to keep going back to Bruce to say we are losing so much money here. We paid so much for Ismail. My background is in accounting and I can juggle any book but at some point you need to put cash in.

"John was capped on a certain amount of money, Bruce and Wayne weren't and they were losing money. They asked me to sell the team unbeknownst to John, they didn't want John to know. So I was out getting perspective buyers and eventually I did lineup TSN who were broadcasters to buy the team and John found out about it, not from me but from someone else. When we had the conversation I said 'John first of all I am only doing what Bruce was telling me to do' and he felt it was a betrayal that One: I didn't tell him and Two: that I would ever consider doing what the other two partners wanted me to do for them. Again I was listening to who was paying my mortgage.

"When somebody crossed John he would write you off I believe. He stopped talking to me. I went back to Wayne and said 'John isn't even talking to me' and Wayne said, 'Don't worry, I will speak to him'."

I talked at length with Cooper, I could see how hard this situation had been for him. It was also apparent how much he loved and respected John. Personally I think John just needed a little time to get over the hurt, I think he would have come around eventually.

Talking to McNall, who knew he was heading for real trouble, when he discussed the sale with John about what was at stake, John understood. "We talked at length about it, we really didn't have any choice but to sell the team, Wayne wanted out too because he wasn't capped either and it had come very expensive. I said 'John I need to sell the team, it's not even up to me.' He was trying to find a group of people to buy the team, but he really couldn't because it didn't make any economic sense. So when were in discussion with TSN (who ended up buying them eventually) they wanted John involved, he knew that, I told him they would want him involved, they would have been crazy not to. For John it wouldn't have changed that much. He was sad about the whole thing but he understood."

John was certainly sad and stressed over this news, but I know he would have made it work.

Meantime, although *Canadian Bacon* hadn't fully wrapped it was pretty much there, John went to Mexico to fulfil another acting obligation. *Canadian Bacon* would be released in 1995 with the closing credit being: "To Johnny LaRue - thanks to you we got our crane shot".

Wagons East

So hear we find ourselves back in Mexico, 1994, on the set of *Wagons East*. I have been dreading writing this chapter. If you didn't know already, the beginning of the book fills you in a little on what happens here and it's just heartbreaking.

The place where John was staying in Durango was found for him by his assistant Bob Crane and Crane's stepfather, Chuck Sloan. It was a "single-story circular home featuring a large living room and satellite bedrooms and baths. It was located in the 'nice section' of Durango, next to a public park that featured only occasional gunfire at night," as Crane described in his book, *Sex, Celebrity and My Father's Unsolved Murder*. 'The Chongos' were staying in the nicest hotel in Durango, the El Presidente, but it wasn't quite private enough for a bona fide movie star.

Crane stayed in Durango until the end of February, then left to go back to Los Angeles to take care of business.

In the book Crane remembers Frankie Hernandez calling him at 7am in the morning, 4th March 1994. Frankie broke the news, he remembers Frankie saying "We went to his house to pick him up to go out to location. There was no answer so we busted the door open and found him in the bedroom". "It looks like a heart attack" Frankie said to Crane, "He must have been sitting on the edge of the bed putting his shoes on. It looked like he'd just fallen backward onto the bed. His feet were on the floor. 'This is un-f**king-believable, Bob!'".

Crane knew that he had to get to Rose Candy and tell her the sad news before the news-reporters did. He met Sloan en route and they drove to the Candy's house in Mandeville Canyon, much to Crane's relief there were no reporters outside the house.

Crane remembers "Rose opened the door. Chuck and I didn't say a word. She looked at Chuck, trying to figure out why he was there with me. Then she looked at me. It took her only a few seconds to work it out. No one said a word. Rose let out the loudest shriek I've ever heard. Chuck and I surrounded her, worried she was going to pass out. We took her back inside, and when she calmed down enough to make sense of it, we told her what Frankie had told us."

Crane went with Rose to St. Martin of Tours, the Catholic school both Jennifer and Christopher were attending.

In 2016 Jennifer and Christopher spoke to *The Hollywood Reporter* about their memories of that sad and fateful day.

Christopher: "I was 9. It was a Friday. I remember talking to him the night before he passed away and he said, 'I love you and goodnight.' And I will always remember that."

Jennifer adds: "I remember my dad the night before. I was studying for a vocabulary test. I was 14. He had just come home for my 14th birthday, which is Feb. 3. So I was talking to him on the phone, and, I hate this, but I was slightly distant because I was studying. So I was like, 'Yeah, OK, I love you. I will talk to you later. Have a great night.' Then I hang up, and I go back to studying."

"They wouldn't tell me what was going on," Jen says.

Chris breaks in, "I have this one memory of seeing this kid in mass, and he is playing around, and I had this weird energy come over me where I was able to feel older. And then Father Donie walked us down to the rectory. Bob Crane, my dad's assistant was there. Our mom was there, in tears."

"And someone says, I don't remember who, 'Your dad has passed away,'" Jen says.

"And we just erupted into tears," Chris adds.

On the day John died a massive piece of amethyst rock he brought his family from Mexico, just suddenly shattered for no reason. Rose told her children it was John's way of saying goodbye.

Back in Durango the actors and the crew were told to stay in their hotel rooms and not speak to anyone who wasn't from the set. Boom operator, Mark Jennings spoke to me about his memories of John and that awful day. "The last three weeks to a month of shooting he was obviously in more and more pain, you could tell cos he would have a way of standing that he was in a lot of discomfort, but he would never complain about it. He never let on as to how much pain he was in. Those last couple of weeks he just seemed tired, just really tired. But he never let it affect his demeanour. He was always smiling. I'm not sure I could have done it, I'm not sure I'm that strong a man to have handled that way.

"The very strange thing was getting driven to the set that morning in the crew van (unaware of what had happened), and I was suddenly sick to my stomach and I couldn't figure out why. We got to the set and all assistant directors were in a really sombre mood. We had a gaffer on the shoot whose name was John who had heart problems. The first AD called us all around and made the announcement that John had died. At first we thought it was our gaffer, that was the first thing that I thought. Then when they said John Candy, just the appal that descended over the entire set, it affected everyone, every single person. They sent us back to the hotel and we were sequestered as journalists had already started to gather. We had a meeting with everyone and just went over what we were going to try and do to get through it.

"The one thing that has stuck with me, the very night before we were doing the opening of the movie, where John is supposedly drunk, we were shooting that whole scene. He's supposed to walk off camera and he walked into the closet instead of the exit he was supposed to go out of, and he utters a line where he says something about wrong room and comes back on camera. I hadn't planted a microphone in that closet to catch that line. It must have been around one in the morning. I said to John, 'I need a favour, can I just get a line from you real quick'. He said to me, 'I'm really sorry Mark, I'm really tired, can we do it tomorrow?' and I said 'Sure, it's just a line and we'll get it tomorrow' and he died that night and we didn't get the line. It's not about me not getting the line, it's about how quickly circumstances can change and from that moment on it has literally affected my life, you don't wait to do things anymore as you just don't know.

"He was probably one of the kindest, gentlest people I have ever known or encountered."

Allegedly, Rose insisted that they didn't do an autopsy on John's body and personally, I can understand why. I am sure John didn't want anyone messing with his body, it was obvious that it was his heart that had gone, and no coroner's report was going to be able to bring him back. For someone that had likely inherited heart problems, for the weight he was carrying, the altitude in Durango, the long days and exhaustion, the pain he was in, the heat - which if he had been sweating - would likely mean his electrolytes were low, I guess everything just added up and that sweet man's heart just had enough. It sounded like it was very quick, literally just sitting on his bed putting his shoes on and then gone.

I once chatted to someone who survived a major heart attack, they actually died at the scene, but luckily for them they were in the middle of an exercise class and the instructors had access to a defibrillator so they managed to get her back. In terms of her recollection, she had none, she wasn't feeling funny beforehand, she could not remember anything about it whatsoever, and for me that was comforting, it was unlikely John knew what was happening, it just happened, he wouldn't have been scared.

For his family and his friends however, they are the ones that really suffered after this. The shock of losing someone you love, without warning, is more than painful or horrific, it is pretty much indescribable. It is hard enough when someone close to you is terminally ill, but eventually you can make peace with the fact they were suffering and although it's still so hard, you console yourself that they are out of pain. When someone literally just disappears overnight, totally unexpected, nothing in the world makes sense anymore. There are literally no words.

John's death was mourned all over the world and still is, to this day. However, he is also celebrated day in day out as the comedic, dramatic actor that he was, an influence to many and still spreading love with his work.

John's funeral was held at St Martin of Tours Catholic Church in Los Angeles. Many remember that day, especially as the police shut down part of the San Diego freeway for the funeral procession, which is totally unheard of, they would usually only do this for the President - that is how much John Candy was respected. The service was a star studded affair, with a eulogy included from his old friend Dan Aykroyd.

The late Tino Insana recalled in an interview that as John's casket was being wheeled down the aisle one of the wheels was making a comedy squeaking noise, other than complete silence you could hear ha-hee... ha-hee... ha-hee... ha-hee... as the casket was wheeled along. Insana inferred that John was there with them, lightening the moment.

John's body was interred in a beautiful resting spot, at Holy Cross Cemetery in Culver City. He is surrounded by marble and being smiled upon by vibrant stained glass windows.

In Toronto, Canada, a memorial service was held by John's Second City Alumni, in St Basil's Church, which was full to the brim with people paying respects. From schoolchildren to senior citizens, the streets were lined with mourners undeterred by the freezing cold temperature and snow. John was even given an honor guard from the Royal Canadian Mounted Police. The service was shown live on TV and Radio.

Catherine O'Hara delivered a eulogy;
""You all have a story" said O'Hara, "You stopped for his autograph and he asked you about you. You carried his bags up to the hotel room and he said, `That's too heavy, let me get that for you.' And then he tipped you."

Mary Margaret O'Hara, Catherine's sister and a critically acclaimed singer songwriter, beautifully performed *Dear, Dark Heart*.

When I interviewed Dave Thomas he told me that he spoke to Dan Aykroyd at John's funeral, they discussed how if you added up every waking hour, John actually lived the life of an 80 year old. "John did everything a lot. John stayed up a lot, John had a lot of friends, John ate a lot, John drank a lot, John loved life and for him, it wasn't possible to get enough of it."

May we all have a life as full as John Candy's - for he did not waste a second.

The final tangent in the Tipton trilogy

Remember Ken Tipton? We left him on the set of *The Flintstones* after taking John Candy's advice. Well a couple of months after John passed away, Tipton finally gets the three vouchers he needs and qualifies for his SAG card. Tipton remembers, "I got it on May 5th 1994, it takes 30 days to process, when it does process you get to union side of casting, you get paid better, you are a professional actor and that was the most important thing. As soon as I was transferred over I got a beep on my pager a few hours later from Central Casting. It said, 'We have a job for you, you will need to go to Universal to be a photo double, you will stand in front of a green screen, they will put you in certain costumes and ask you to stand in certain positions and here is your contact, the time etc.' All I knew I was going to be a photo double insert for something."

Ken drives into the Universal Studios parking lot as a professional actor going to his first professional gig, feeling positive as his career is on a much brighter path.

"They had a fake bar, a stable, a couple of horses and a green screen set up. They were going to put me in digitally later". The costume lady comes in to see Tipton and she says they are going to have to pad him out a bit, she brings him leather trousers, chaps, a big leather coat, a shirt, and a big hat. "I tried it on and it was loose, so they put some padding in my jacket - I didn't know who I was playing. This costume smelt like shit, it smelt like it had just come off the range, but it also had a human scent to it like someone had been wearing it. I asked, 'Where did you get this jacket?' I was already sweating in it, so whoever else had warn it must have been sweating big time. They said 'that's the jacket John Candy wore in a movie called *Wagons East!*', much to Tipton's shock, 'What? I am wearing John Candy's coat?', they replied, 'Yeah you are the photo double insert for John Candy.'

"John didn't know me for shit, but he was a nice guy in St Louis and he was a nice guy letting me call him and just because he was a nice guy I got to earn my SAG card. I'm from Missouri, I don't see this karma stuff, in Missouri the motto is 'show me', here in California they talk about karmic stuff.

"I don't know how much more karmic you can get, than a chance meeting with a guy in St Louis in a trailer when you're an asshole, that leads to a phone call, leads to you earning you a screen actors guild card and you doing your first professional acting job as replacing him (John) in a movie. It was very cool."

As Tipton recalled this story to me I began to cry, I felt like John had said "here, have your first proper job on me", some would call it a crazy coincidence, I like to think of it as John working his magic, because that was exactly the type of thing he would have done.

John's children have grown up successful, talented and a credit to both John and Rose. Both Jennifer and Christopher have gone into acting following their father's footsteps, but they also have other creative interests too. Jennifer runs a show at Second City Hollywood called *Couch Candy* where she interviews her cool aunties and uncles about their time at Second City and also about working with her dad, like her mum she is also an artist. Christopher has his own radio show called *Neuz Pollution* on *KXLU* and is the lead singer in a band called *Chotto Ghetto*.

John has taught me so much about life and how we can go on living afterwards, about working hard, loving harder and how to treat people.

I said it at the beginning of this book and I will say it again at the end...

Legends like John Candy never really die.

Thank you, John. Love... love is not a big enough word.

Filmography (Dates of release)

1973   Class of '44

1975   It Seemed Like a Good Idea at the
Time

1976   Tunnel Vision

            The Clown Murders

            Find The Lady

1978   The Silent Partner

1979   Lost and Found

            1941

1980   Double   Negative   (aka   Deadly
Companion)

            The Blues Brothers

1981   Stripes

            Heavy Metal

1982   It Came from Hollywood

1983   National Lampoon's Vacation

            Going Berserk

1984   Splash

Only the Lonely

Delirious

Career Opportunities

JFK

1992   Once Upon a Crime

            Boris and Natasha: The Movie

1993   Rookie of the Year

            Cool Runnings

1994   Wagons East

            Hostage For a Day (TV Movie)

1995   Canadian Bacon

Selected Bibliography

Thomas, Dave, SCTV Behind the Scenes, 1996, Canada, M&S

Patinkin, Sheldon, The Second City: backstage at the world's greatest comedy theatre, 2000, USA, Sourcebooks

Thomas, Mike, The Second City: Unscripted, 2009, USA, Villard Books

O'Leary, Jim and Parrish, Wayne, Double Blue: an illustrated history of the Toronto Argonauts), 2007, Canada, ECW Press

McCrohan, Donna, The Second City: A Backstage History of Comedy's Hottest Troupe, 1987, USA, Perigree Books

Knelman, Martin, Laughing on the Outside: The Life of John Candy, 1996, Canada, Viking Press

McNall, Bruce, Fun While It Lasted, 2003, USA, Hyperion Books

McNall, Bruce, Fun While It Lasted, 2003, USA, Hyperion Books

Mankiewicz, Tom and Crane, Robert, My Life As A Mankiewicz, 2012, USA, University Press of Kentucky

Mulligan, Terry David, Mulligan's Stew, 2011, Canada, Heritage House

O'Hara, Maureen, T'is Herself, 2005, UK, Simon & Schuster UK

Crane, Robert, Crane: Sex, Celebrity, and My Father's Unsolved Murder, 2017, USA, University Press of Kentucky

Websites

www.johncandy.com

www.imdb.com